BABE RUTH'S
Incredible Records and the 44 Players Who Broke Them

John A. Mercurio

SPI BOOKS

A division of Shapolsky Publishers, Inc.

Also by John A. Mercurio

**Major League Baseball Records
Official Profiles of Baseball Hall of Famers
Boston Red Sox Records
New York Yankee Records**

THE INCREDIBLE
MAJOR LEAGUE
BASEBALL

RECORDS OF
BABE RUTH

AND ALL THE PLAYERS WHO BROKE THEM

BILL TERRY	ROBERTO CLEMENTE
PIE TRAYNOR	BILLY MARTIN
PAUL WANER	TONY LAZZERI
PEPPER MARTIN	BILL DICKEY
FRANKIE FRISCH	DOUG DECINCES
ARKY VAUGHN	JACKIE ROBINSON
AL SIMMONS	FRANK CROSETTI
HANK AARON	EARLE COMBES
GABBY HARTNETT	REGGIE JACKSON
STAN MUSIAL	ROGER MARIS
BEN CHAPMAN	DUKE SNIDER
WHITEY FORD	MICKEY MANTLE
PAT DUNCAN	JOE MEDWICK
JOE CRONIN	ALLIE REYNOLDS
DEL UNSER	HANK BAUER
CHUCK KLEIN	CHARLIE KELLER
EARL AVERILL	JOHNNY MIZE
ROGERS HORNSBY	YOGI BERRA
HOOT EVERS	BABE HERMAN
JIMMIE FOXX	TED WILLIAMS
TY COBB	ALLIE REYNOLDS
CHARLIE GEHRINGER	JOE DIMAGGIO

*Babe Ruth's Incredible Records
and the 44 Players Who Broke Them*

S.P.I. BOOKS
A division of Shapolsky Publishers, Inc.

Copyright © 1993 by John Mercurio

ISBN 1-56171-221-3

For any additional information, contact:

S.P.I. BOOKS/Shapolsky Publishers, Inc.
136 West 22nd Street
New York, NY 10011
212/633-2022 / FAX 212/633-2123

PRINTED IN CANADA

10 9 8 7 6 5 4 3 2 1

To my wife, Jean, who hung in there with me for all
these wonderful years.

                              Thanks, hon'.

CONTENTS

Preface

What Is A Record Profile? 12

RECORD PROFILES

1. Babe Ruth 13
2. Hank Aaron.. 44
3. Roger Maris 49
4. Ty Cobb... 58
5. Lou Gehrig 66
6. Joe DiMaggio 71
7. Stan Musial.. 75
8. Rogers Hornsby 80
9. Ted Williams 84
10. Jimmie Foxx 88
11. Chuck Klein 91
12. Babe Herma.. 94
13. Johnny Mize... 98
14. Pepper Martin 103
15. Joe Cronin...106
16. Bill Dickey 110
17. Frank Crosetti 113
18. Charlie Gehringe 116
19. Ben Chapman 120
20. Duke Snider 123
21. Red Ruffing...127
22. Charlie Keller 130
23. Mickey Mantle 133

24. Reggie Jackson 136
25. Whitey Ford 141
26. Hank Bauer 144
27. Roberto Clemente 147
28. Joseph Medwick 150
29. Jackie Robinson 154
30. Hoot Evers 159
31. Bill Martin 162
32. Wesley Ferrell 165
33. Del Unser 168
34. Gabby Hartner 171
35. Frankie Frish 175
36. Yogi Berra 179
37. Al Simmons 184
38. Arky Vaughn 187
39. Bill Terry 190
40. Allie Reynold 194
41. Earl Combs 197
42. Pie Traynor 200
43. Earl Averil 204
44. Paul Waner 208
45. Tony Lazzerie 212

Bibliography 216

Photo Credits 217

RECORD PROFILES
STATISTICS, ANALYSIS AND LORE

COMPILED BY JOHN A. MERCURIO

PREFACE

Babe Ruth has long been considered baseball's greatest player. But was he the absolute greatest? Was he the greatest all-around player in baseball history? Or was he the greatest home run hitter or batter?

As can be seen by the above questions, when seeking the answer as to who was the greatest, the question "Greatest what?" should be asked first. Are we looking for the greatest all-around player, or the greatest home run hitter, or the greatest batter? Could it be possible that Babe Ruth was the greatest in all three categories?

How is greatness determined? In the case of a non-pitcher, is it by his highest batting or slugging average? Or are his home runs and RBIs more important categories to consider? How about his defensive skills? Are we looking for the total player, who helps his team both at bat and in the field?

This book will attempt to answer some of these questions. This writer (and researcher) takes the liberty of giving his opinion that the greatest player is determined by those who have the most talent with which to help their team win ball games – meaning that great players are those who can help win ball games in many ways. This should eliminate the good-bat no-glove man and vice versa.

We are looking for the complete player, one who can hit, run, throw, and field. We are also looking for the players who have established the most records. But not just any records. We are looking for players who have created records that have stood the test of time. In addition, we are looking for players who are heads and shoulders above the rest, those who are league leaders in both the batting and fielding departments. When all these are considered and combined, we have established some concrete evidence that will separate the men from the boys.

Who are the players who have created the most records? Which players have had the longest-standing records? Who are the players who possess the skills to set records both at bat and in the field? What players have led the league the most times in batting average, fielding average, slugging average, home runs, RBIs, runs scored, total bases, and extra bases?

When trying to determine baseball's greatest players, where do we start? With whom do we start?

Since Babe Ruth carries the reputation as baseball's greatest player (or one of baseball's greatest players), this writer takes the liberty of starting with him and then comparing the achievements of all the others against him. But before this can be done we must know about the research that has been conducted by this writer, allowing him to substantiate any and all of his claims.

ABOUT THE AUTHOR

John A. Mercurio has been researching baseball records for the last 12 years. He has published four previous baseball books and has recorded every season and career record of every player in baseball history in chronological order. These records begin in 1876, the first year of baseball, and show all records in batting, pitching, and fielding. Every player who has ever held or set a record is profiled and the complete history of every major record category is also included.

With this accomplished, the author was able to count the exact number of records each player had created and thus produce an individual record profile on every player. This is a great start, allowing valuable comparisons to be made among players.

The next research that he did was to find out who the league leaders were, and who were the greatest among these leaders. When this was accomplished, a hunt took place seeking the most outstanding players who were record setters and league leaders in both batting and fielding. With this information in the bank, the author is ready to make his findings known to the baseball world. And those findings are that Babe Ruth has established more records and has led the league in more categories than any player in baseball history. But the author is going to let you decide, after reading this book, if Babe Ruth is truly baseball's greatest player. Good luck.

EXPLANATION OF A RECORD PROFILE

WHAT IS A RECORD PROFILE?

A record profile is a chronological listing of every record created by a player. In addition to telling the exact number of records each player has established, it shows specifically what those records were.

The profile shows how many years a record lasted before it was broken, and by whom it was broken. It also tells of the records that have been tied and who tied them. Last, it informs us about all records that have never been broken.

The record profile consists of five columns. The first column on the left gives the year or years the record was established. The second column shows the category of each record. The third column lists the numbers achieved by the player. The fourth column provides the number of years the record has lasted before being broken, while the last column reports the players who have tied or broken the record and also depicts an unbroken record by stating "Never broken" in bold print.

The value of a record profile is that for the first time in baseball history we may know how many records each player has established during his career. It allows for the comparing of one player's records with another's. It serves as as one of the excellent methods of determining baseball's greatest players. It provides information that previously was unavailable and unknown to the baseball world. It can be one of the means used in rating and ranking players.

The record profile contains all league records – American, National and Major Leagues – as well as All-Star games and World Series marks. It includes rookie records and manager's records. It includes game records, season records, and career records in batting, pitching, and fielding. Some profiles may include club records as well.

RECORD PROFILE

GEORGE HERMAN RUTH

(Babe, The Sultan of Swat, The Bambino)
b. Feb. 6, 1895, d. Aug. 16, 1948
BOS-AL 1914-19, NY-AL 1920-34, BOS-NL 1935

Number Of Records Established–206 (1st)

American League Records

Season Batting Records		Years lasted before broken		Broken by:
1915	Most Home Runs by Pitcher	4	16	Wesley Farrell
1918	Highest Home Run %	3.5	1	Self
1919	Most Home Runs	29	1	
	Highest Home Run %	6.7	1	Self
1920	Most Home Runs	54	1	Self
	Highest Home Run %	11.8		**Never broken**
	Most Extra Base Hits	99	1	Self
	Highest Slugging Average	.847		**Never broken**
	Most Base on Balls	148	3	Self
1921	Most Home Runs	59	6	Self
	Most Extra Base Hits	119		**Never broken**
	Most Total Bases	457		**Never broken**

	Most Runs Scored	177		**Never broken**
	Most RBIs	171	6	Broken by Lou Gehrig
1923	Most Bases on Balls	170		**Never broken**
1927	Most Home Runs	60	34	Broken by Roger Maris

Season Batting Title Records

1921	Most Home Run Titles	4	2	Self
	Most Home Run % Titles	4	1	Self
1923	Most MVP Titles	1	1	Tied by many
	Most Home Run Titles	5	1	Self
	Most Home Run % Titles	6	1	Self
	Most RBI Titles	4	3	Self
1924	Most Home Run Titles	6	2	Self
	Most Home Run % Titles	7	2	Self
	Most Runs Scored Titles	5	2	Self
1926	Most Home Run Titles	7	1	Self
	Most Home Run % Titles	8	1	Self
	Most Slugging Average Titles	8	1	Self
	Titles Most RBI Titles	5	2	Self
	Most Runs Scored Titles	6	1	Self
	Most Bases on Balls Titles	5	1	Self
1927	Most Home Run Titles	8	1	Self
	Most Home Run % Titles	9	1	Self
	Most Slugging Average Titles	9	1	Self
	Most Runs Scored Titles	7	1	Self
	Most Bases on Balls Titles	6	1	Self
1928	Most Home Run Titles	9	1	Self
	Most Home Run % Titles	10	1	Self
	Most Slugging Average Titles	10	1	Self
	Most Total Bases Titles	6		Tied by Ty Cobb and Ted Williams
	Most RBI Titles	6		**Never broken**
	Most Runs Scored Titles	8		**Never broken**
	Most Bases on Ball Titles	7	1	Self
1929	Most Home Run Titles	10	1	Self
	Most Home Run % Titles	11	1	Self
	Most Slugging Average Titles	11	1	Self

1930	Most Home Run Titles	11	1	Self
	Most Home Run % Titles	12	1	Self
	Most Slugging Average Titles	12	1	Self
	Most Bases on Balls Titles	8	1	Self
1931	Most Home Run Titles	12		Never broken
	Most Home Run % Titles	13		Never broken
	Most Slugging Average Titles	13		Never broken
	Most Bases on Balls Titles	9	1	Self
1932	Most Bases on Balls Titles	10	1	Self
1933	Most Bases on Balls Titles	11		Never broken

Season Fielding Records

1919	Least Errors-LF	2	31	Hoot Evers
	Highest Fielding Average	.992	24	Charlie Keller
1923	Most Putouts-RF	378	48	Del Unser
	Most Total Chances-RF	409	48	Del Unser

Career Batting Records 1914 - 34

	Most Home Runs	708		Never broken
	Highest Home Run %	8.5		Never broken
	Most Extra Base Hits	1350		Never broken
	Most RBIs	2199		Never broken
	Highest Slugging Ave.	.690		Never broken
	Most Bases on Balls	2,036		Never broken
	Most Strikeouts	1,306	34	Mickey Mantle

Career Batting Title Records 1914 - 34

	Most Home Run Titles	12		Never broken
	Most Home Run % Titles	13		Never broken
	Most Total Base Titles	6		Tied by Ty Cobb and Ted Williams
	Most Runs Titles	8		Never broken
	Most RBI Titles	6		Never broken
	Most Bases on Balls Titles	11		Never broken
	Most Slugging Average Titles	13		Never broken

Major League Records

Season Batting Records

1915	Most Home Runs By Pitcher	4	16	Wesley Ferrell
1919	Most Home Runs	29	1	Self
	Highest Home Run %	6.7	1	Self

1920	Most Home Runs	54	1	Self
	Highest Home Run %	11.8		**Never broken**
	Highest Slugging Average	.847		**Never broken**
	Most Extra Base Hits	99	1	Self
	Most Bases on Balls	148	3	Self
1921	Most Home Runs	59	6	Self
	Most Extra Base Hits	119		**Never broken**
	Most Total Bases	457		**Never broken**
	Most RBIs	171	6	Lou Gehrig
1923	Most Bases on Balls	170		**Never broken**
1927	Most Home Runs	60	34	Roger Maris

Season Batting Title Records

1923	Most Home Run Titles	5	1	Self
	Most RBI titles	4	3	Self
	Most MVP Titles (Non-Pitcher)	1	10	Jimmie Foxx
	Most Home Run % Titles	6	1	Self
1924	Most Home Run Titles	6	2	Self
	Most Home Run % Titles	7	2	Self
	Most Runs Scored Titles	5	2	Self
1926	Most Home Run Titles	7	1	Self
	Most Home Run % Titles	8	1	Self
	Most Slugging Titles	8	1	Self
	Most RBI Titles	5	2	Self
	Most Runs Scored Titles	6	1	Self
	Most Bases on Balls Titles	5	1	Self
1927	Most Home Run Titles	8	1	Self
	Most Home Run % Titles	9	1	Self
	Most Slugging Average Titles	9	1	Self
	Most Runs Scored Titles	7	1	Self
	Most Bases on Balls	6	1	Self
1928	Most Home Run Titles	9	1	Self
	Most Home Run % Titles	10	1	Self
	Most Slugging Average Titles	10	1	Self
	Most Total Base Titles	6	1	Rogers Hornsby
	Most RBI Titles	6		**Never broken**
	Most Runs Scored Titles	8		**Never broken**
	Most Bases On Balls Titles	7	2	Self

1929	Most Home Run Titles	10	1	Self
	Most Home Run % Titles	11	1	Self
	Most Slugging Average Titles	11	1	Self
1930	Most Home Run Titles	11	1	Self
	Most Home Run % Titles	12	1	Self
	Most Slugging Average Titles	12	1	Self
	Most Bases on Balls Titles	8	1	Self
1931	Most Home Run Titles	12		Never broken
	Most Home Run % Titles	13		Never broken
	Most Slugging Average Titles	13		Never broken
	Most Bases on Balls Titles	9	1	Self
1932	Most Bases on Balls Titles	10	1	Self
1933	Most Bases on Balls Titles	11		Never broken

Season Fielding Records

1923	Total Chances	409	7	Chuck Klein

Career Batting Records 1914-35

	Most Home Runs	714	41	Hank Aaron
	Highest Home Run %	8.5		Never broken
	Most Extra Base Hits	1,356	28	Stan Musial
	Most RBIs	2,211	41	Hank Aaron
	Highest Slugging Average	.690		Never broken
	Most Bases on Balls	2,056		Never broken
	Most Strikeouts	1,330	33	Mickey Mantle

Career Batting Title Records 1914-35

	Most Home Run Titles	12	Never broken
	Most Hone Run % Titles	13	Never broken
	Most Total Base Titles	6	Rogers Hornsby
	Most Runs Scored Titles	8	Never broken
	Most RBI Titles	6	Never broken
	Most Bases on Balls Titles	11	Never broken
	Most Slugging Average Titles	13	Never broken

All-Star Game Records

Game Batting Records

1933	Games Played	1	1	Self with many
	Hits	2	1	Al Simmons

	Home Runs	1	8	Arky Vaughn
	Total Bases	5	4	Lou Gehrig, Joe Medwick
	Extra Base Hits	1	1	Al Simmons, Earl Averill
	Runs Scored	1	1	Frankie Frisch, Al Simmons
	RBIs	2	1	Joe Medwick, Earl Averill
	Strikeouts	2	1	Lou Gehrig
1934	Games Played	2	1	Pepper Martin Paul Waner, Pie Traynor, Bill Terry Gabby Hartnett, Ben Chapman, Charlie Gehringer, Lou Gehrig, Al Simmons and Joe Cronin
	Strikeouts	3	33	Roberto Clemente

Career Batting Records   1933-34

Games Played	2	1	*See above*
At Bats	8	1	Al Simmons
RBIs	2	4	Lou Gehrig
Bases on Balls	2	4	Charlie Gehringer
Strikeouts	5	4	Lou Gehrig

World Series Records

Game Batting Records

1923	Home Runs	2	3	Self
1926	Home Runs	3		Tied by self and Reggie Jackson
	Total Bases	12		Tied by self and Reggie Jackson
	Runs Scored	4		Tied by Earle Combs, Frank Crosetti and Reggie Jackson

	Bases on Balls	4		Tied by Jackie Robinson and Doug DeCinces
1928	Home Runs	3		Tied by Reggie Jackson
	Total Bases	12		Tied by Reggie Jackson
1932	RBIs	4	4	Tied by Bill Dickey and Tony Lazzeri

4-Game Series Batting Records

1927	Home Runs	2	1	Lou Gehrig
	RBIs	7	1	Lou Gehrig
1928	Extra Base Hits	6		**Never broken**
	Runs Scored	9		Tied by Lou Gehrig
	Hits	10		**Never broken**
	Batting Average	.625		**Never broken**
	Total Bases	22		**Never broken**

6-Game Series Batting Records

1923	Home Runs	3	54	Reggie Jackson
	Extra Base Hits	5	54	Reggie Jackson
	Total Bases	19	30	Billy Martin
	Runs Scored	8	54	Reggie Jackson
	Bases on Balls	8		**Never broken**
	Slugging Average	1.000	54	Reggie Jackson

7-Game Series Batting Records

1926	Home Runs	4		Tied by Duke Snider, Hank Bauer and Gene Tenace
	Bases on Balls	11		Tied by Gene Tenace
	Slugging Average	.900	26	Johnny Mize

Career Batting Records 1914 - 35

Games Played	41	2	Frankie Frisch
At Bats	129	2	Frankie Frisch
Hits	42	2	Frankie Frisch
Home Runs	15	32	Mickey Mantle

Home Run %	11.6	**Never broken**
Runs Scored	37 31	Yogi Berra
RBIs	33 6	Lou Gehrig
Total Bases	96 31	Yogi Berra
Extra Base Hits	22 32	Mickey Mantle
Bases on Balls	33 32	Mickey Mantle
Slugging Average	.744 49	Reggie Jackson
Strikeouts	30 27	Duke Snider
Series Played	10 31	Yogi Berra
Consecutive Games Hit Safely	13 25	Hank Bauer

World Series Fielding Records

4-Game Series-RF

1927	Putouts	10	Tied by Ival Goodman

World Series Pitching Records

Game Records

1916 Most Innings	14	**Never broken**

5-Game Series Pitching Records

1916 Fewest Hits	6 33	Allie Reynolds

6-Game Series Pitching Records

1918 Shutouts	1	Tied by many

Career Pitching Records 1914 - 35

Scoreless Innings	29⅔ 44	Whitey Ford
Fewest Hits/9 Innings	5.52 2	Sherry Smith
Lowest ERA	0.87 28	Harry Brecheen

Career Fielding Records-RF   1914 - 35

Putouts	46 26	Hank Bauer
Total Chances	49 26	Hank Bauer

Summary

Babe Ruth's 206 league records are more than any player's in baseball history. He broke his own records 55 times, 17 of his records have been tied, 51 have never been broken, and the remaining 138 records have been broken by 44 different players. (Their names appear on the first page.)

In addition to these phenomenal feats, the great Bambino compiled 69 batting titles, which are also more than any players in baseball history. And while a member of the New York Yankees, he accumulated an unbelievable total of 246 club records, by far the most of any player in Yankee history.

Does this make the Babe the greatest all-around player who ever played the game? You can be sure, there has never been a player who could do all the things that Ruth did. There may have been a more frequent contact hitter, better defensive players and more outstanding pitchers; but to find all three of these qualities in one player is extremely rare.

Babe Ruth was more than just a great player. He was the man who is credited with saving the game of baseball. After the infamous Black Sox scandal of 1919, baseball reached its lowest ebb. It was the Babe who made the fans forget all that and brought them back to fill the ball parks. This he did before too much cynicism could seriously affect the game. He roared onto the scene with feats of heroism that were totally without precedent.

Not only did he help save baseball, not only was he the myth upon which the Yankee dynasty was created, but he single-handedly changed the way the game was played. By his prodigious home runs, he ended the bunt and slap era of Ty Cobb.

Babe Ruth came to the New York Yankees as a gift from Boston Red Sox owner Harry Frazee. Frazee was a show business producer, and each time one of his plays fizzled, he sold off one of his players to keep himself afloat.

Ruth was sold to the Yankees in 1919 for the sum of $125,000. This was a lot of money in those days, but a drop in the bucket when compared to the money he earned for the Yankees as he filled the park day after day, year after year.

The Babe was unique, one of a kind, and there could never be another like him. The man was a combination of ballplayer, personality, magnetism, show business, drama, and innocence that had to have been hand-crafted by some celestial artisan who is probably too pleased to want to top himself and too wise to try.

Postseason Awards

1923 MVP

Career Batting Statistics

Years: 22
Strikeouts: 1,330
Home Run %: 8.5 (1st)
At Bats: 8,399
Slugging Average: .690 (1st)
RBIs: 2,211 (2nd)
Doubles: 506
Pinch Hits: 13
Stolen Bases: 123
Home Runs: 714 (2nd)
Games: 2,503
Batting Average: .342
Runs: 2,174 (2nd)
Hits: 2,873
Pinch Hit at Bats: 67
Walks: 2,056 (1st)
Triples: 136

Career Pitching Statistics

Years: 10
Shutouts: 17
Games Completed: 107
Losses: 46
Relief Wins: 2
Hits Allowed: 974
ERA: 2.28
Relief Losses: 2
Strikeouts: 488
Games Started: 148
Wins: 94
Relief Games: 15
Innings: 1,221
Winning Percentage: .671
Saves: 4
Walks: 441
Total Games: 163

CHRONOLOGICAL HIGHLIGHTS OF
BABE RUTH'S LIFE

Feb. 6, 1895	Birthday.
June 13, 1902	Sent to St. Mary's Industrial School for Boys at age 7.
June, 1910	Brother Matthias realizes Babe's talents as a baseball player and spends many hours pitching to him, hitting him ground balls and fly balls.
Mar. 2, 1914	Jack Dunn, owner of the Baltimore team, signs Babe to his first contract, for $600 per season. Dunn becomes Babe's legal guardian since Babe is only 19 years old and was in custody of St. Mary's until age 21.
Mar. 2, 1914	Babe takes his first train ride to spring training in Fayetteville, N.C.
Mar. 23, 1914	Pitches in relief against first major league team, the Philadelphia Phillies.
Mar. 30, 1914	Completes 9 innings against the champion Philadelphia Athletics.
Apr. 13, 1914	Loses to the New York Giants 3 - 2.
Apr. 16, 1914	Hits two long drives over Casey Stengel's head for home runs.
Apr. 22, 1914	Shuts out Buffalo 6 - 0 on 2-hitter.
Apr. 25, 1914	Offered $10,000 bonus and salary to play with the new Federal League. Jack Dunn kills the deal. Increases Babe's salary to $1,800 per season.
June 27, 1914	Defeats Buffalo 10 - 5. He is now becoming famous for his great pitching and hitting long home runs.
July 10, 1914	Sold to the Boston Red Sox and is now earning $625 per month.
July 11, 1914	Gets first big league win against Cleveland 4 - 3. It had taken him four months to get into the major leagues.
Aug. 20, 1914	Sent to Providence R. I. farm team to help them win their pennant as the Red Sox had no chance of winning theirs.

Sept. 5, 1914	Hits first professional home run with Providence.
Sept. 27, 1914	Called back up to the Red Sox.
Oct. 2, 1914	Gets first major league hit, a double against Len Cole of the New York Highlanders (Yankees).
Oct. 18, 1914	Marries Helen Woodford, a waitress. For 15 years he thinks her name was Woodring.
May 16, 1915	Hits first major league home run at Polo Grounds off Jack Warhop of the New York Yankees.
July 21, 1915	Hits longest home run ever seen, at Sportsman Park in St. Louis. It crashes through a window of a Chevrolet dealer across the street from the park.
Aug. 1915	Strikes out Ty Cobb, Sam Crawford, and Bobby Veach in succession. He was as popular a pitcher as would be Sandy Koufax and Tom Seaver.
Sept. 1915	Completes first season with 18 - 8 record and helps the Red Sox win the pennant.
Oct. 1915	Sets a record of sorts by being sent in as a pinch hitter for a regular player. A pitcher batting for a player was unheard of. (He lined out.) (In 1915 World Series, Red Sox defeat Phillies 4 games to 1; Babe does not get a chance to pitch.)
June 1916	Hits first pinch-hit home run.
Sept. 1916	Leads American League with 1.75 ERA and has a record of 23 - 12. Helps Red Sox to another pennant. Leads league in games started, with 41, and shutouts, with 9.
Oct. 1916	Pitches first World Series game; sets record by going 14 9-inning games and winning 2 - 1.
Apr. 1917	Salary increased to $5,000 per season.
June 23, 1917	Punches umpire and is suspended one week and fined $100. This is the game in which he walked the first batter and was ejected and Ernie Shore replaced him; the

runner was thrown out stealing and Shore retired the next 26 batters in a row for a perfect game.

Sept. 1917   Has another fine year, winning 24 and losing 13 while leading the league in complete games with 35. He has 40 hits and a .325 batting average with 2 home runs.

Apr. 1918   Salary is boosted to $7,500.

Sept. 1918   Is now performing as half pitcher and half player. Wins 13 and loses 7. Ties Tillie Walker for the home run title with 11, gets 95 hits, and hits .300. Helps Boston win another pennant.

Sept. 5, 1918   Babe pitches 1 - 0 shutout in first game of World Series.

Sept. 9, 1918   Wins fourth game 3 - 2. Before 2 runs are scored against him in 8th inning, he has set a new scoreless innings record of $29\frac{2}{3}$ innings. This record will last four decades before it is broken by Whitey Ford.

Sept. 9, 1918   Gets his first World Series hit, a triple that drove in two runs and gave the Red Sox a 2 - 0 lead in game four.

Apr. 1919   Signs 3-year contract for $27,000 per year.

Apr. 10, 1919   Hits 579-foot home run against New York Giants in exhibition game.

Apr. 18, 1919   Hits 4 home runs in one game against Baltimore in exhibition game, and 2 homers the next day. He had been honored for the first time in a pre-game ceremony by his friends in Baltimore from St. Mary's School.

Sept. 20, 1919   Declared "Babe Ruth Day," at Fenway Park. Babe is now a full-time player but helps injury-riddled staff by appearing in 17 games, winning 9 and losing 5. As a batter, he sets new home run record with 29. He also leads the league in home run percentage (6.7) runs scored (103), RBIs (114), and slugging average (.657). He bats .322 with 139 hits.

Dec. 26, 1919	Babe is sold to the New York Yankees for $125,000 and Boston owner Harry Frazee is given a $350,000 loan. This represents the largest sale of a single player.
Jan. 5, 1920	Signs a 2-year contract for $40,000 per season.
Mar, 1920	Runs off a heckler in spring training who pulls a knife on him.
Apr. 1920	Knocks himself out by running into a palm tree during a spring training game.
Aug. 20, 1920	Signs to do film entitled, *Headin' Home*. Filmed in Haverstraw, N.Y. Gets $15,000 in advance and $35,000 in royalties.
Sept. 1920	Ruth's popularity makes Yankees first team to draw more than one million fans in one season. The attendance was 1,289,422, almost double that of 1919. His popularity also helps fans forget about the 1919 Black Sox scandal of fixing the 1919 World Series, which had threatened the games existence.
Sept. 1920	Babe enjoys finest season, setting new home run record with 54 and leading the league in home run % (11.8), runs (158), RBIs (137), bases on balls (148), and in slugging average (.847) while batting .376.
Oct. 1920	Colonel Jacob Ruppert, the team owner, buys the land to build Yankee Stadium.
Oct.-Nov. 1920	Babe earns $90,000 on barnstorming tour.
Feb. 21, 1921	Signs with agent Christy Walsh, who makes Babe rich by getting numerous promotions and endorsements.
Apr. 1921	Put in jail one day for speeding violation.
May 1921	Hits 550-foot home run in St. Louis.
July 2, 1921	Hits his 132nd career home run, breaking the record of Roger Connor.
Sept. 1921	Sets new home run record with 59. Leads league in home run %, runs (177), RBIs (171), bases on balls (144), and slugging average (.846) while batting .378.
Oct. 1921	Scientists conduct series of tests on Ruth and determine he is "super-human." They

find his coordination of eye, brain, nerve system, and muscle 90% compared to 60% for the average man. His eyes are 12% faster, ears 10% faster, and his nerves steadier than 499 out of 500 persons. His attention and quickness of perception are $1\frac{1}{2}$ times above average and his quickness and accuracy 10% above normal.

Oct. 5, 1921	Babe is allowed to coach third base in first World Series game against Giants. He singles first time up, steals second and third on the next two pitches. Yanks win 3 - 0.
Oct. 6, 1921	Tears up his elbow attempting to steal third. Yanks win 3 - 0.
Oct. 7, 1921	Re-injures elbow attempting to steal second and is forced to leave game in 8th inning. (Yanks lose, 13 - 5.)
Oct. 9, 1921	Elbow, serverely infected, causes fever but Babe hits home run; Yanks lose 4 - 2.
Oct. 10, 1921	Doctors say he should be in hospital because infection is spreading throughout his body. But Babe plays in spite of this, plus a pulled muscle. Lays down surprise bunt to start game-winning rally.
Oct. 11, 1921	Babe is unable to play because of infection, fever, and injuries. Giants win series.
Oct. 28, 1921	Signs contract to do 20-week vaudeville show for $3,000 per week. He is touted as the "Superman of Baseball."
Oct. 15 - 21, 1921	Goes on barnstorming campaign against Commissioner Landis' wishes. (He was not given permission to go on tour.) Is fined his World Series share of $3,362 and is suspended for the first month of the 1922 season.
Apr. 1922	Babe becomes highest-paid player in baseball history by signing for $52,000.
May 4, 1922	Has tonsils out.
May 25, 1922	Babe goes into stands after heckler, who runs like hell. Is fined $200 and removed

	as team captain.
June 19, 1922	Suspended five days for threats made to umpire Bill Dineen.
July 17, 1922	In publicity stunt, Bob Meusel drops ball from roof of theater building for Ruth to catch.
Aug. 13, 1922	Babe is operated on for abcess on calf of left leg.
Aug. 30, 1922	Suspended three days for vulgar and vicious language to umpire.
Sept. 1922	It is discovered that Babe has a daughter who was born on June 7, 1921. It had been covered up because she was not healthy, was a premature birth, and weighed only $2\frac{1}{2}$ pounds. It was later found that this baby was adopted from a home and was not Babe's natural daughter.
Oct. 1922	Ruth again leads Yankees to pennant, belting 35 homers, leading the league in home run % (8.6) and in slugging average at .672.
Oct. 1922	On this day the first World Series is broadcast by radio directly from the ball park. The announcer is Grantland Rice. Yanks lose four straight to the Giants as Ruth suffers at bat, managing only two weak hits, going hitless in the last three games, and compiling a meager .118 batting average.
Nov. 15, 1922	Ruth is honored guest at Baseball Writers dinner. The guest speaker is Senator Jimmy Walker, who will later go on to become mayor of New York. Walker stuns the crowd and the Babe when he rips into him by saying he is a poor example to the children of America, who look up to him and worship him. Babe is embarrassed and comes to tears, vowing he will stop his late-night carousing and drinking and get into shape for the next season.

Mar. 1923	Babe is sued by Dolores Dixon for fathering her child. This suit is later dropped.
Apr. 18, 1923	Opening day at new Yankee Stadium. Crowd of 74,000 fills stadium while 25,000 more are turned away. Babe reports in, in the best shape of his life at 209 pounds. Ruth hits first Yankee Stadium home run. Writer Fred Lieb decides to call Yankee Stadium "The House That Ruth Built." The right field stands will soon be called "Ruthville."
Apr. 19, 1923	Babe hits 450-foot triple, and now the *New York American* newspaper begins daily column following his at bats. The column is called "The Truth on Ruth."
May 1923	Babe meets showgirl Claire Hodgson and begins five-year courtship. This will ultimately lead to his wife Helen's nervous breakdown.
Sept. 1923	Babe wins first MVP award, belts 41 homers, leads league in home run percentage, runs, RBIs, bases on balls, and slugging average while batting .393. Is hailed as baseball's greatest batsman. Leads Yanks to another pennant.
Oct. 10, 1923	Casey Stengel's inside-the-park home run with two out in the ninth wins game for the Giants (game one).
Oct. 11, 1923	Ruth's two home runs lead Yanks to victory, but his longest drive is caught by Casey Stengel in center field (game two).
Oct. 12, 1923	Casey Stengel is again hero in game three by hitting home run over Ruth's head into the right-field bleachers. Giants win, 1 - 0.
Oct. 13 - 15	Yankees win next three games and their first World Series. Ruth stars with 3 home runs, 1 double, 1 triple, scoring 8 runs, driving in 3, and batting .368. More than 300,000 paid $1,063,815 to see six games. It was the first one-million-dollar series. The Babe is the idol of all kids in America.

Apr. 1924	Babe again reports in in great shape at 218 pounds.
Sept. 1924	Leads league in home runs, home run %, runs, bases on balls, batting and slugging averages, but Washington wins pennant behind the outstanding pitching of Walter Johnson. Babe Ruth and Charlie Chaplin voted America's two most widely known celebrities.
Apr. 17, 1925	Suffers the "bellyache that is heard around the world." Has fainting spells, fever, chills, etc. Is operated on for an abcess many believed was part of a sexual disease. It was called the "mystery malady." Wife Helen has nervous breakdown.
June 1, 1925	Babe returns to lineup. Wally Pipp complains of headache and is replaced by Lou Gehrig.
Aug. 28, 1925	Babe is fined $5,000 and suspended by Miller Huggins for misconduct off the field. It it the largest fine ever imposed upon a player.
Sept. 1925	Ruth ends season with worst year ever. He only manages 25 homers, 104 hits, and he bats .290.
Nov. 1925	Brother Matthias of St. Mary's tries to soothe Babe's spirits and save his marriage. Babe in return buys him a new Cadillac which is soon wrecked by a train. So the Babe buys him another one. Babe embarks on a campaign of "repentance."
Dec. 1925	Yankees hire Artie McGovern, gym owner, to get Ruth into shape. He is successful in reducing Ruth's weight by 23 pounds, his waist from $48\frac{1}{2}$ to $39\frac{3}{4}$, his hips from 46 to 40 inches, and even his neck from 17 to 16 inches.
July 1926	Babe hits 602-foot homer in Detroit.
Sept. 1926	Leads Yankees to pennant and league with 47 homers, and in home run percentage, runs, RBIs, bases on balls, and slugging

average while batting .372. (For the next six years he will average 50 home runs, 147 runs scored, and 156 RBIs.)

Oct. 2, 1926   Game one, scores winning run on Lou Gehrig's single.

Oct. 3, 1926   Game two, the great Cardinal pitcher Grover Alexander retires the last 21 Yankees in order to help the Cardinals defeat the Yankees 6 - 2.

Oct. 6, 1926   Babe sends autographed ball to an ailing 11-year-old boy named Johnny Sylvester along with a note which says, " I will try to hit a home run for you." Doctors had given the boy only a short time to live, but upon hearing Babe Ruth hitting 3 home runs in the fourth game of the World Series, the boy responds "miraculously" and goes on to live a long life. (The two were eventually united on Babe's farewell ceremony at Yankee Stadium in April 1947.)

Oct. 10, 1926   Cardinals defeat Yankees in game seven to win the series, 4 games to 3. The Babe gets his fourth home run of the series.

Nov. 1926   Babe Ruth and Lou Gehrig go on barnstorming tour with a team called "The Busting Babes."

Jan. 1927   Babe signs contract for $100,000 to do 12-week vaudeville show and a Hollywood movie called *The Babe Comes Home*.

Apr. 1927   Opening Day, Babe reports in, in fine shape at 224 pounds, thanks to the training from Artie McGovern. Signs 3-year contract for $70,000 per season. Remains the highest-paid player in baseball history. (The average player was earning $7,000.)

Sept. 1927   Babe leads the Yankees to another pennant by hitting 60 home runs, and continues to place many records in the book. Again he is the leader in home run percentage, runs, bases on balls, and slugging average. He bats .356 and drives in 164 runs. This is the

team that was called "Murderers' Row,"
which many consider the greatest team in
baseball history. As a team they batted .307.

Oct. 5, 1927   Game one, Babe gets three hits to aid
                Yankees' 5 - 4 win.

Oct. 7, 1927   Game three, Babe hits 3-run homer to ice
                game for Yanks 8 - 1.

Oct. 8, 1927   Yankees take the Pirates in four straight
                games as Ruth hits 2-run homer. Game is
                actually won on a wild pitch in the bottom
                of the ninth. Ruth bats .400 on 6 hits,
                2 home runs, and 7 RBIs. This is first
                World Series to be broadcast nationally.

Nov. 1927   Barnstorming tour now consists of the
                Bustin' Babes and Lou Gehrig's
                "Larrupin' Lou's." Ruth earns $70,000.

Mar. 1928   Has his book published, entitled *Babe
                Ruth's Own Book of Baseball.*

Sept. 1928   Enjoys another fine season leading
                Yankees to another pennant. This time he
                is the league leader in home runs, home
                run percentage, runs, RBIs, bases on balls,
                and slugging average while batting .323.

Oct. 4 - 9   Yankees take four straight from the
                Cardinals as Ruth and Gehrig star. Gehrig
                has 4 homers and Babe 3. Babe gets all
                three in game four. Babe has 10 hits and
                bats .625, driving in 4 runs while scoring 9.

Jan. 12, 1929   Babe's wife Helen dies in a house fire
                when overcome by smoke and fumes.
                Helen's sister Dora thinks foul play is
                involved and orders autopsy to see if
                Helen was poisoned. Rumors had it that
                Helen wanted a divorce and $100,000 from
                the Babe.

Jan. 16, 1929   Autopsy report shows that Helen died
                from smoke and fumes and case is closed.
                At the funeral, Babe weeps profusely.

Mar. 1929   In Yankee spring training they are given
                numbers for the first time. They are num-
                bered according to their place in the

batting lineup. Thus Ruth, batting third, got number three.

Apr. 17, 1929   Marries Claire Hodgson, whom he had loved for many years. This was on opening day after the game had been rained out. She places on him many restrictions which the Babe abides by. He claims he is now a family man. Claire begins the practice of going on road trips with him, which Yankee management thinks a great idea because it keeps the Babe on his best behavior.

June 1929   Becomes ill and misses two weeks playing.

Aug. 11, 1929   Hits his 500th home run.

Sept. 25, 1929   Yankee manager Miller Huggins dies. Babe asks to become manager but is turned down.

Oct. 1, 1929   Yankees do not win pennant, but Babe has another outstanding season, again leading the league in home runs, home run %, and slugging average while batting .345.

Oct. 29, 1929   Stock market crashes.

Winter 1930   Babe signs 2-year contract for $80,000 per year. He also makes $200,000 on endorsements and promotions. This is remarkable, considering the nation was experiencing the Great Depression.

May 21, 1930   Hits 3 home runs in one game.

Oct. 1, 1930   Babe cannot lead the Yankees to the pennant but he still leads league in home runs, home run percentage, bases on balls, and slugging average while batting .359. He again is turned down as Yankee manager. Joe McCarthy is hired.

Oct. 1, 1931   Yanks finish third as Ruth connects for his 600th career home run. Babe unhappy with McCarthy's restrictions. Babe leads league for the last time in home runs, home run percentage, and slugging average while batting a super .373. It is a year in which the Babe earned more money than President Hoover. The Babe was quoted as saying, "I had a better year than Hoover."

March 1932
Ruth holds out because he is asked to take a pay cut. This after the year before hitting 46 homers and batting .373. But the Depression was making it difficult for everyone, so Babe gives in and settles for $75,000.

Oct. 1932
Another fine season ends as Babe hits 41 homers and bats .341, leading the Yankees into their tenth World Series.

Sept. 28 - Oct. 2, 1932
Yanks take four in a row from the Chicago Cubs. Ruth has 5 hits, which include 2 home runs, giving him a total of 15 for his career and making him the highest producer of World Series home runs in baseball history. He also scores 6 runs and drives in 6 runs, setting records in these categories as well.

This is the series in which the Babe pointed to center field and hit his famous "called shot." Ruth himself later said he never pointed toward center field but that he was telling the Cub players that "it only takes one for me to hit the ball out of the park." This was after he deliberately took the first two strikes, raising one finger on the first strike and two fingers on the second strike. He did intend to hit the next pitch out of the park and, when he did, he muttered to himself, "Lucky, lucky, lucky."

March 1933
Signs for $52,000 and is still the highest-paid player in baseball.

Sept. 1933
His skills fading, the Babe still manages 34 home runs and hits .301. Pitches the last game of the season, wins 6 - 5 and hits a home run.

Oct. 1933
Babe is again rejected as Yankee manager. Other clubs turn him down also.

March 1934	Signs for $35,000. His total earnings since 1914 have been $918,477, not counting the income from outside endorsements and promotions.
June 1934	Begins his own radio show three times a week. He is placed between "Tom Mix" and "Amos and Andy."
July 13, 1934	Hits his 700th career homer.
July 14, 1934	Receives his 2,000th base on balls. It is estimated that over the years he has walked to first a distance of 34 miles.
Sept. 25, 1934	Plays last game for the Yankees in Yankee Stadium.
Oct. 1, 1934	Plays last game for the Yankees in Washington where he was honored by his friends from St. Mary's School.
Oct. 1934	Babe again is rejected as Yankee manager.
Nov. 1934	Barnstorms to Japan and enjoys a four-month European vacation.
Feb. 1935	Boston Braves sign Babe to 3-year contract as player, assistant manager, and vice-president at $35,000 per year. It is a stunt tied to increasing gate receipts. Babe quits at the end of the season, but not before blasting 3 home runs in one game. (May 25, 1935.)
June 1938	Signs $15,000 contract to be a coach for the Brooklyn Dodgers.
Sept. 1938	Quits Dodgers when Leo Durocher becomes manager instead of him.
Jan. 13, 1939	Colonel Jacob Ruppert dies. On his deathbed, calls Ruth "Babe" for the first time. He had always called him "Root," his German accent for Ruth.
July 4, 1939	Yankees give Lou Gehrig a farewell ceremony, as he is dying from a rare disease. Babe fights away the tears as the two great sluggers embrace.
July 11, 1939	The Babe is inducted into the Hall of Fame with the very first group of players which include Ty Cobb, Christy Mathewson, Honus Wagner, and Walter Johnson.

July 1940	Ruth challenges Ty Cobb to a charity golf match. Cobb wins a 2-of-3 match.
Nov. 1940	Ruth offered $25,000 to play himself in a movie about Lou Gehrig called *Pride of the Yankees*. Gary Cooper played the role of Gehrig.
Aug. 23, 1942	Babe and Walter Johnson team up to put on a hitting exhibition for the Army - Navy Relief Fund. A crowd of 69,000 fans jam Yankee Stadium to see the Babe deposit several home runs into "Ruthville." His last blast was a mighty one that reached far back into the third tier of the upper deck, an area that few players have ever reached.
Mar. 1944	Japanese troops charge American lines, yelling, "The hell with Babe Ruth."
Apr. 2, 1944	Babe takes part in a wrestling match as a referee.
June. 1944	Babe bowls against New York football Giants' Ken Strong in a benefit for the March of Dimes. He gives so much of his own money to this event that he has to borrow cab fare to get home.
May 16, 1946	Flies to Mexico to support the Mexican Baseball League.
Jan. 15, 1947	Doctors discover he has cancer. Twenty-seven thousand get-well letters are received.
Mar. 1947	Pulls in 50-lb. sailfish while resting and vacationing in Florida.
May. 1947	Ford Motor Company names Babe Ruth head of American Legion Baseball Leagues. Claire and Babe travel 50,000 miles promoting the league.
Apr. 1947	Baseball Commissioner Happy Chandler declares "Babe Ruth Day," at Yankee Stadium. One of the guests is Johnny Sylvester, the boy who miraculously recovered when Babe hit a home run for him. Sylvester is now 32 years old.

June 25, 1947	Babe returns to the hospital. Agrees to allow unproven drug to be used on him. Improvement is made and Babe is soon released.
July, 1947	Allied Artists signs Ruth to a $150,000 contract for the rights to a book and movie called *The Babe Ruth Story*. William Bendix plays the part of the Babe.
June 13, 1948	Ruth is a guest at 25th Anniversary of Yankee Stadium. Using a bat as a cane, he makes a brief speech and then unashamedly embraces Ed Barrow, who has been like a father to him.
Aug. 13, 1948	Babe is back in hospital, now in critical condition. Many ball players come to cheer him up. One is Connie Mack, the famous manager of the Philadelphia Athletics. The Babe says to Mack, "The termites have got me."
Aug. 15, 1948	Babe kisses Claire good-bye, tells her he won't be able to kiss her tomorrow, for he will not be there.
Aug. 16, 1948	At 8:01 a. m. baseball's greatest player is dead. Not since the death of President Roosevelt has the loss of a single American so moved the nation. More than 75,000 fans pay their last respects.

Quotes From Babe Ruth

"It's a gift." (When asked about his hitting ability).

"All I can tell 'em is pick a good one and sock it. I get back to the dugout and they ask me what it was I hit and I tell 'em I don't know, except it looked good."

"I was listed as an incorrigible, and I guess I was. Looking back on my early boyhood, I honestly don't remember being aware of the difference between right and wrong."

"Hot as hell, ain't it Prez?" (The Babe said to President Harding upon being introduced on a sweltering, hot day).

"I have only one superstition. I make sure to touch all the bases when I hit a home run."

"Hello, Mr. Mack. The termites have got me." (Said an ailing Babe to Connie Mack, not long before Ruth's death from cancer).

The Nicknames Of Babe Ruth

Babe Ruth has been referred to by more names than any player in baseball history. Below is a list of them.

1. The Sultan of Swat
2. Zorba
3. The Bambino
4. Prince of Pounders
5. Wizard of Wham
6. Bazoo of Bang
7. Maharajah of Maul
8. Nigger Lips
9. Nigger
10. Rube Waddell in the rough
11. Big Baboon
12. Ape
13. Monkey
14. Tarzan
15. Two-Head
16. Caveman of Baseball
17. The Boston Terror
18. Mastodonic Mauler or Mauling Mastodon
19. The Diamond Studded Ball Buster
20. The Billion Dollar Fish
21. The Behemoth of Bust

22. A Modern Beowolf
23. Mauling Monarch
24. The Rajah of Rap
25. Mauling Menace
26. A Dauntless Devastating Demon
27. The Human Howitzer
28. His Royal Nibs
29. The Wondrous Walloper
30. Superman
31. The Colossus of Rhodes (Big Bruiser)
32. Jidge
33. Chief Big Bat
34. The Abraham Lincoln of Baseball
35. The God of Baseball
36. Pot Belly
37. Balloon Head
38. Czar of Clout
39. El Sultan del Bat
40. El Rey Jonronero

Babe Ruth The Practical Joker

The Babe loved to play practical jokes. Here are some of the things he loved doing:

1. Stuffing a lit cigarette down someone's pants.
2. Stuffing a small player into his locker and leaving him there as he left for the field.
3. Smashing straw hats.
4. Nailing smoking pipes to the wall.
5. Nailing shoes to the floor.
6. Planting a smoke bomb in a friend's car.
7. Handing a slimy fish to a doorman.
8. Slipping a rubber balloon under someone who is about to sit down, producing the sound of passing gas.

Little Known Facts About Babe Ruth

1. He hated to wear underwear, collars, and ties.
2. He never choked up on the bat with two strikes.
3. He hated to wear sliding pads.
4. He had a bootlegger in every town.
5. He once thought "amnesia" was an after-dinner drink.
6. His season home runs were often more than the combined total of an entire team. (In 1920, the combined total of 14 teams did not equal the number of home runs Babe hit.)
7. His favorite radio program was "The Lone Ranger."
8. He ate at least three or four times more than the average person.
9. He spoke the German language well.
10. He claimed his mother hated him.
11. He chewed tobacco before he was 10-years-old.
12. He loved to play hooky from school.
13. He was a trained shirt-maker.
14. He began as a left-handed catcher.
15. He stole from his father's cash register to buy his friends ice cream.
16. He was always first in line for breakfast.
17. He thought nothing of climbing back into soiled underwear after a game.
18. He would use his roommate's toothbrush.
19. He was an outstanding base stealer.
20. He owned a 160-acre farm in New England.
21. As a rookie, he had his bat sawed in half by veteran players.
22. He was partner in his father's saloon.
23. He considered leaving baseball to become a prize fighter.
24. He owned a cigar company.

25. He had Mafia connections, was Al Capone's guest, and was invited to many of their parties.

26. He was considered "super-human" by a team of scientists at Columbia University.

27. He caught a ball dropped from an airplane.

28. He was a frequent guest at the White House, especially during the Harding administration.

29. He was a big gambler and once bet $18,000 on a horse in a race. (He lost.)

30. He admited to losing over $250,000 in gambling. He had bookies in every town.

31. He had a portable Victrola that he took everywhere with him.

32. He could hit a golf ball 300 yards. But he didn't know which direction it would go.

33. He never played a night game.

34. He lost and gained over $2\frac{1}{2}$ tons of weight during his career.

35. He introduced cabbage-head air conditioning, placing cabbage leaves taken from ice cooler under one's baseball cap to keep one's head cool on hot summer days.

36. His bats were called "Black Betsy," "Big Bertha," and "Beautiful Bella."

37. He was investigated in the death of his first wife by the Boston District Attorney.

38. He allowed his second wife (Claire) to control him. He abided by her restrictions.

39. He tried desperately to get a job as a major league manager, but there were no takers.

40. His salary represented about 40% of the Yankee payroll.

41. He loved to play cards. Poker and bridge were his favorites.

42. He had his own radio show and did many vaudeville acts.

43. After he retired, he was never given a free pass to Yankee Stadium by the Yankees.

44. He established more records than any player in baseball history.

45. He had more unbroken records than any player in baseball history.

46. He led his league in various batting categories more times than any player in baseball history.

47. He swung the heaviest bat of any player (46 ounces).

Known Facts About Babe Ruth

1. He loved kids.

2. He visited hospitals and signed thousands of photos and baseballs for charities.

3. He sold war bonds during the World War II.

4. He smoked cigars.

5. He was a big drinker.

6. He loved the ladies.

7. He loved parties, and was the life of the party.

8. He was very boisterous.

9. He saved the game of baseball.

10. He was one of baseball's greatest batsmen.

11. He was the highest-paid player of his era.

12. He was an outstanding pitcher.

13. He changed the game of baseball from bunts and singles to home runs.

14. He loved life and lived it to the fullest.

15. He didn't get along well with his managers.

16. He broke curfew most of the time.

17. He had a candy named after him.

18. He grew up in an orphanage.

19. He was sold to the Yankees by the Red Sox.

20. He hit the longest home runs of any player in his era.

How Babe Ruth Got His Nickname

Researchers are not sure how Babe Ruth got his nickname. Three possibilities considered are:

1. When he was taken to St. Mary's School at the age of seven, he was crying so hard, he was called a "baby."

2. When he was led into his first spring training camp by Jack Dunn, the players yelled out, "Look at Dunn's new babe."

3. When he was tearing around town on a "borrowed" bike a newsman would say, "He is the biggest babe of the lot."

Babe Ruth himself says he thinks it started when he first walked into his first spring training camp.

Babe's Own Names For People

He was terrible at remembering names and would call people, "Kid," "Doc," or "Stud." Any woman under 35 was "sister," and if any older, she was called "mom."

He had some pet names for some of his teammates as well. Tony Lazzeri was "Wop," Benny Bengough was called "Barney Google,"and others were called "chicken neck," "flop-ears," "runt," and "rubber-belly."

RECORD PROFILE

HENRY LOUIS AARON

(Hank, Hammerin' Hank)
b. Feb 5, 1934
Mil-NL 1954-65, Atl-NL 1966-74, Mil-AL 1975-76

Number of Records Established – 21

National League Records

Season Batting Records	Years lasted before broken		Broken by
1966 RBI Titles	4		Tied Cap Anson, Honus Wagner, Sherry Magee, & Rogers Hornsby
1967 Total Base Titles	7	2	Self
1969 Total Base Titles	8		**Never broken**
Career Batting Title Rececords 1954-74			
RBI Titles	4		Tied Cap Anson, Honus Wagner, Sherry Magee and Rogers Hornsby
Total Base Titles	8		**Never broken**

Career Batting Records 1954-74

At Bats	11,628	12	Pete Rose
Runs Scored	2,107		Pete Rose
Home Runs	733		**Never broken**
RBIs	2,202		**Never broken**
Games Played	3,076		Pete Rose
Extra Base Hits	1,453		**Never broken**
Total Bases	6,587		**Never broken**

Major League Records

Season Batting Title Records

1967	Total Base Titles	7	2	Self
1969	Total Base Titles	8		**Never broken**

Career Batting Records 1954-76

Games Played	3,298	7	Carl Yastrzemski
At Bats	12,364	10	Pete Rose
Home Runs	755		**Never broken**
Extra Base Hits	1,477		**Never broken**
Total Bases	6,856		**Never broken**
RBIs	2,297		**Never broken**

Career Batting Title Records 1954-76

Total Base Titles	8	**Never broken**

A YEAR-BY-YEAR CHART OF BABE RUTH'S AND HANK AARON'S HOME RUN RECORDS

BABE RUTH			HANK AARON		
Year	Number of Years	Totals	Year	Number of Years	Totals
1914	0	1	0	1954	13	1	13
1915	4	2	4	1955	27	2	40
1916	3	3	7	1956	26	3	66
1917	2	4	9	1957	44	4	110
1918	11	5	20	1958	30	5	140
1919	29	6	49	1959	39	6	179
1920	54	7	103	1960	40	7	219
1921	59	8	162	1961	34	8	253

Year	Number of Years		Totals	Year	Number of Years		Totals
1922	35	9	197	1962	45	9	298
1923	41	10	238	1963	44	10	342
1924	46	11	284	1964	24	11	366
1925	25	12	309	1965	32	12	398
1926	47	13	356	1966	44	13	442
1927	60	14	416	1967	39	14	481
1928	54	15	470	1968	29	15	510
1929	46	16	516	1969	44	16	554
1930	49	17	565	1970	38	17	592
1931	46	18	611	1971	47	18	639
1932	41	19	652	1972	34	19	673
1933	34	20	686	1973	40	20	713
1934	22	21	708	1974	20	21	733
1935	6	22	714	1975	12	22	745
				1976	10	23	755

Total At Bats: 8,399   Total At Bats: 12,364
Home Run %: 8.5   Home Run %: 6.1

Summary

Who was the greater home run hitter between Babe Ruth and Hank Aaron? Does the above chart give a clear answer? Statistics alone do not tell the complete story. Perhaps if these two outstanding home run hitters played in the same era and under similar conditions, statistics could provide an answer. But because they played in two extremely different eras and because Babe Ruth played his first four years as a pitcher and half pitched and played in his fifth year, it is very difficult to come to a strong conclusion.

The different eras referred to, Babe Ruth's 1914 - 35 and Hank Aaron's 1954 - 76, were as different as night and day. Babe Ruth played with a "dead ball" from 1914 to 1919. The Babe did not have to face the tough relief pitching that existed in Aaron's era. In Aaron's favor was the fact that he had 3,965 more at bats. Would Ruth have hit more homers than Aaron if he had the same at bats? Would

Ruth have hit modern-day relief pitching as well as Aaron? Obviously, these questions can never be answered; thus no definitive conclusion can be drawn.

In attempting to determine who the greater all-around player was, a close look can be taken in other departments.

Babe Ruth		Hank Aaron	
Strikeouts	1,330	Strikeouts	1,383
Hits	2,873	Hits	3,771 (3rd)
Doubles	506	Doubles	624 (8th)
Triples	136	Triples	98
Runs	2,174 (2nd)	Runs	2,174 (2nd)
RBIs	2,211 (2nd)	RBIs	2,297 (1st)
Walks	2,056 (1st)	Walks	1,402
Steals	123	Steals	240
Batting Average	.342	Batting Average	.305
Slugging Average	.690 (1st)	Slugging Average	.555

It appears that Aaron was a better contact hitter, based upon his lesser number of strikeouts per at bats. Aaron only struck out 53 times more than Ruth but had 3,965 more at bats.

During Ruth's career, the average league batting average was a strong .282 compared to the league average during Aaron's era, which was only .255. Because there are always two sides to every argument, one could say the batters in Ruth's day were superior to those in Aaron's time. The other side of the story is that the difference in averages was due to the difficult relief pitching of modern times. The differences in league averages are 27 points, and if that were added to Aaron's batting average it would bring him up to .332 compared to Ruth's .342.

In Ruth's favor are the numbers, which, amazingly, have him tied with Aaron in runs scored even though Aaron had 3,965 more at bats. Also amazing is that Ruth had almost as many RBIs in his fewer at bats. Could this be due to the weaker pitching during Ruth's era or was he just a better producing hitter than Aaron? Or was Ruth's production a result of his playing on championship teams, with more men getting on base than Aaron's weaker teams? Experts could argue these points for an eternity without coming to any intellectual agreements. Now let's take a quick look at the two players' defensive skills.

Both were outfielders with strong arms. Both could run well and possessed better than average speed. Ruth had a fielding average of .964 compared to Aaron's .975. But even this statistic cannot be taken on face value. The gloves of Aaron's day were far superior to the skimpy glove that barely covered Ruth's hand. And no one knows how difficult or easy the official scorers were in those early years. So no sensible conclusion can be drawn here either. Ruth led the league in fielding average only once, while Aaron led the league in completing double plays three times, but he was never a league leader in fielding average.

RECORD PROFILE

ROGER EUGENE MARIS
b. Sept. 10, 1934 d. 1984
Cle-Al. 1957-58, KC 1969, NY-AL 1960-66, StL-NL 1967-68

Number of Records Established–10

American League Records

Season Batting Records	Years lasted before broken	Broken by
1961 Most Home Runs	61	**Never broken**

Career Fielding Records-RF 1957-66		
Fielding Average	.985 21	Dwight Evans

Major League Records
Season Batting Records

1961 Most Home Runs	61	**Never broken**

New York Yankee Club Records
Season Batting Records

1961 Most Home Runs	61	**Never broken**

Season Fielding Records-RF

1963 Fewest Errors	2 2	Tied self

1964	Fewest Errors	1	2	Tied self
	Fielding Average	.996		**Never broken**
1966	Fewest Errors	1		Tied by Johnny Callison

Career Fielding Records-RF 1957-66

Fewest Errors/Year	3.3		Never broken
Fielding Average	.985		**Never broken**

Roger Maris will always be famous as the man who broke Babe Ruth's home run record for one season. Overshadowed by his picture-perfect home run swing was the fact that this great slugger was an outstanding outfielder. It was a rare occasion when he would get his glove on a ball and then drop it. Muffing balls whether in the air or on the ground was not part of his routine. Roger Maris was one of baseball's most outstanding defensive right fielders. He possessed a powerful and accurate arm, and when he left the American League at the end of the 1966 season, he owned the record, for the highest fielding average for right fielders. Eight years later, Al Kaline would tie this record, and it wasn't until 1987 that Dwight Evans of the Boston Red Sox posted a slightly higher fielding average. In all, Maris' record stood for twenty-one years.

The New York Yankees had many great right fielders during the history of their franchise. First there was "Hit 'em where they ain't" Willie Keeler, then Babe Ruth, George Selkirk, who replaced the Babe, "Old Reliable" Tommy Henrich, and Hank Bauer. None of these great players could match Maris's glove. When research was completed to determine the player who averaged the fewest errors per year, it was Maris who came out on top. When the highest career fielding averages were compiled, again it was Maris.

Maris began his career with the Cleveland Indians in 1957. He went to Kansas City in the middle of the 1958 season and completed the 1959 season with them before coming to the Yankees in 1960. In that year Maris gave a hint of what was to come when he led the league in home run % with a hefty 7.8, which produced 39 homers. Little did the baseball world know that this was just the beginning of something big. Also in that 1960 season, Maris led the league in RBIs with 112 and slugging average with a .581. This earned him the MVP award.

Going into the 1961 season, the talk was about Mantle and Maris, as they were being touted as the greatest 1 - 2 home run combination since Babe Ruth and Lou Gehrig. The entire season was centered upon Mantle and Maris and neither of them disappointed the fans. Yankee attendance reached a new high that year, for how could the fans stay away as these two great sluggers tore enemy pitchers apart? If it wasn't Mantle hitting a home run one game, it was Maris, and vice versa.

By the end of July, Maris had 40 home runs and Mantle 39. They were both on a pace with the mighty Babe and the excitement grew more and more each day. But Maris was not enjoying it very much. Coming from a small town, Fargo, in North Dakota, he was never comfortable in the big city, and particularly so when his batting feats attracted the sharks and piranhas of the press, radio, and television. He became moody, sullen, and angry. He could never understand why the press kept asking him the same questions over and over again.

Besides the press giving him fits, certain elements among Yankee rooters never, for some inexplicable reason, fully accepted him, despite the exciting, hustling qualities he brought to the game. Perhaps it was because he was trampling on Ruthian soil, or perhaps it was because there was only room for one hero in New York and Mantle was already their favorite. Whatever the reason, Maris, while having one of the most fabled seasons in baseball history, became increasingly unhappy as it went on.

On September 1, Maris was fast approaching Ruth's record with 51 round trippers and Mantle had dropped behind with 48. With the tension rising day by day, hate mail accumulated in the Maris mailbox. Many death threats were received; that was how stupid some people were. Maris, understandably, was a nervous wreck. How he even completed the season was a miracle in itself. Driven to distraction, he came near to a breakdown. His hair fell out in clumps, he hid from his interrogators when he could escape, and gave surly answers when he could not.

In the midst of all this excitement, baseball Commissioner Ford Frick and American League President Joe Cronin got into a hot dispute. Frick had stated that if Maris hit more home runs than Ruth it would not count, because of the new 162-game schedule. Cronin insisted that it should count. Most of the fans seemed to agree with the Commissioner and, as it turned out, he would have the last word.

Nevertheless, the two sluggers kept swinging. By game number 134, Maris was up to 53 while Mantle was still stuck at 48. At this same point, Ruth had hit only 49 home runs. By game 148, Maris had now reached 56 homers, but he was now only one game ahead of Ruth's pace. He connected for his 57th homer in game 150 and hit one more the next game. He had now tied the marks of Jimmie Foxx in 1932 and Hank Greenberg in 1938. Maris got his 59th homer in game 154, and because of Frick's ruling, Ruth's record was still intact. The fans settled back to see what Maris could do in the remaining games. Four games later, he hit number 60 – and that's the way it stayed until the very last game of the season.

Tracy Stallard was on the mound for the Red Sox and the tension mounted each time Maris came to the plate. Maris failed in his first at bat, but in the fourth inning, there it was, that picture-perfect home run swing. Roger had connected and history was made. But did he have the record? Frick said he wouldn't give it to him, and never did. The saddest part of this story is that Roger Maris went to his grave without ever officially being given the most prized record in all baseball.

Maris died at an early age from cancer. Many doctors attribute cancer to stress. Could it be possible that the stress Maris endured during his 1961 season was a prime cause contributing to his death? If this is so, it makes the story even sadder.

But Roger Maris would eventually he recognized as the man who broke Babe Ruth's season home run record. He wasn't alive to see it, but in 1991, baseball Commissioner Fay Vincent officially sanctioned Roger Maris's 61 home runs as the new record.

Maris did win the MVP award in 1961, becoming one of the few who had won the award two years in a row. During Maris's first five years with the Yankees, he was a main reason why the team had won five consecutive pennants and two World Series championships. In 1967, he was traded to the St. Louis Cardinals and helped them win the pennant in that year and also in 1968. In all, Maris played in seven World Series, coming to bat 152 times with 33 hits and 6 home runs; also drove in 18 runs and scored 26 runs. Only five players have scored more runs in World Series play than he.

Postseason Awards

1960 MVP
1961 MVP

Career Statistics

Years: 12:
Home Runs: 275
Games: 1,463
Batting Average: .260
Runs Scored: 826
Hits: 1,325
Pinch Hit at Bats: 99
Walks: 652
Triples: 42

Strikeouts: 733
Home Run Percentage: 5.4
At Bats: 5,101
Slugging Average: 476
RBIs: 851
Doubles: 195
Pinch Hits: 23
Stolen Bases: 21

GAME BY GAME HOME RUN CHART OF RUTH & MARIS HOME RUN RACE

	BABE RUTH			ROGER MARIS	
Home Runs	Game	Date	Home Runs	Game	Date
1	4	Apr.15	1	11	Apr. 26
2	11	23	2	17	May 3
3	12	24	3	20	May 6
4	14	29	4	29	May 17
5	16	May 1	5	30	19
6	16	1	6	31	20
7	24	10	7	32	21
8	25	11	8	35	24
9	29	17	9	38	28
10	33	22	10	40	30
11	34	23	11	40	30
12	37	28	12	41	31
13	39	29	13	43	June 2
14	41	30	14	44	3
15	42	31	15	45	4
16	43	31	16	48	6
17	47	June 5	17	49	7
18	48	7	18	52	9
19	52	11	19	55	11
20	52	11	20	55	11
21	53	12	21	57	13
22	55	16	22	58	14
23	60	22	23	61	17
24	60	22	24	62	18
25	70	30	25	63	19
26	73	July 3	26	64	20
27	78	8	27	66	22
28	79	9	28	74	July 1

Home Runs	Game	Date	Home Runs	Game	Date
29	79	9	29	75	2
30	83	12	30	75	2
31	94	24	31	77	4
32	95	26	32	82	9
33	95	26	33	82	9
34	98	28	34	84	13
35	106	Aug. 5	35	86	15
36	110	10	36	92	21
37	114	16	37	95	25
38	115	17	38	95	25
39	118	20	39	96	26
40	120	22	40	97	26
41	124	27	41	106	Aug. 4
42	125	28	42	114	11
43	127	31	43	115	12
44	128	Sept. 2	44	116	13
45	132	6	45	117	14
46	132	6	46	118	15
47	133	6	47	119	16
48	134	7	48	119	16
49	134	7	49	124	20
50	138	11	50	125	22
51	139	13	51	129	26
52	140	13	52	135	Sept. 2
53	143	16	53	135	2
54	147	18	54	140	6
55	148	21	55	141	7
56	149	22	56	143	9
57	152	27	57	151	16
58	153	29	58	152	17
59	153	29	59	155	20
60	154	30	60	159	26
			61	163	Oct. 1

Babe Ruth **1927 Season Statistics**		**Roger Maris** **1961 Season Statistics**	
Games	151	Games	151
AB	540	AB	590
H	192	H	159
2B	29	2B	16
3B	8	3B	4
HR	60	HR	61
HR%	11.1	HR%	10.3
R	158	R	132
RBI	164	RBI	142
BB	138	BB	94
SO	89	SO	67
SB	7	SB	0
BA	.356	BA	.269
SA	.772	SA	.620

Summary

Upon closely examining the home run race on a day-by-day and a game-by-game comparison, it is surprising to see how far ahead Roger Maris was for most of the season.

The Babe got off to a faster start, getting his first homer in game four while Maris did not connect until game eleven. Both sluggers went almost a week without a homer, but then they both began to hit them with consistency. Eight times Ruth had two home runs in one day; six of those times it was two homers in one game, while the other two times they were double headers. Maris hit two home runs in one day seven times, and they were all in double headers.

Strangely, both sluggers hit two homers on the same date in a double-header on July 26.

The Bambino hit his 10th homer in game 33, while Maris did not get his 10th until game 40. Maris closed the gap slightly during the next 10 homers, reaching the 20 mark in game 55, while Babe was there in 52 games.

Ruth hit a 10-game slump between games 60 and 70 that allowed Maris to catch up and pass him as he was getting a home run on almost a daily basis. Between game 55 and 66, Maris hit 12 homers to gain a tie with the Babe, but at this point Ruth had played 78 games. Maris stayed ahead of Ruth's pace from game 63 to game 152. It was at this time, when Maris had 58 homers, that pitchers gave him nothing good to hit. No pitcher wanted to go down in history as the one who gave up the 61st home run. In addition, Maris was receiving death threats and verbal abuse from fans who did not want to see the record broken. The press was on him continuously as Roger was looking for places to hide. It was difficult for him to sleep or get any rest; the pressure was unbelievable.

When looking at the season statistics, Ruth outhit Maris in every category except home runs. But most will admit that the conditions of 1927 were nowhere close to the conditions of 1961. Babe Ruth only had the pressure of breaking his own record. Maris had to struggle against his legend, the fans, and the pitchers. The Babe did not have to face the relief pitching, as did Maris, and this, in addition to all else, is what makes Maris's feat one of the greatest records in baseball history.

Quotes From Roger Maris

"I don't want to be Babe Ruth. He was a great ballplayer. I'm not trying to replace him. The record is there and damn right I want to break it, but that isn't replacing Babe Ruth."

"It would have been a helluva lot more fun if I had never hit those sixty-one home runs. All it brought me was headaches."

"Look at this. My goddam hair is coming out. Did your hair ever fall out from playing baseball?"

RECORD PROFILE

TYRUS RAYMOND COBB
(Ty, The Georgia Peach)
b. Dec. 18, 1886, d. July 17, 1961
Det-AL 1905-26, Phi-AL 1927-28
Manager Det-AL 1921-26

Number of Records Established-146 (2nd)

American League Records

Season Batting Records		Years lasted before broken	Broken by:
1909	Stolen Bases	76 1	Eddie Collins
1911	Hits	248 9	George Sisler
	Singles	169 9	George Sisler
	RBIs	144 10	Babe Ruth
	RBIs per Game	0.98 10	Babe Ruth
	Stolen Bases	83 1	Clyde Milan
1915	Stolen Bases	96 65	Rickey Henderson
Season Batting Title Records			
1908	Total Bases	2 1	Nap Lajoie
	Hits	2 1	Self
	RBIs	2 13	Self

1909	Triple Crown	1	38	Ted Williams
	Batting Average	3	1	Self
	Slugging Average	3	1	Self
	RBIs	3	2	Self
	Hits	3	2	Self
	Stolen Bases	2	2	Self
1910	Batting Average	4	1	Self
	Slugging Average	4	1	Self
	Runs Scored	2	1	Self
1911	Hits	4	1	Self
	Singles	3	1	Self
	Total Bases	4	4	Self
	Runs Scored	3	4	Self
	RBIs	4	15	Babe Ruth
	Stolen Bases	3	4	Self
	Batting Average	5	1	Self
	Slugging Average	5	1	Self
	MVP Award	1	13	Walter Johnson
1912	Hits	5	3	Self
	Singles	4	3	Self
	Batting Average	6	1	Self
	Slugging Average	6	2	Self
1913	Batting Average	7	1	Self
1914	Batting Average	8	1	Self
	Slugging/Average	7	3	Self
1915	Hits	6	2	Self
	Singles	5	2	Self
	Total Bases	5	2	Self
	Runs Scored	4	1	Self
	Stolen Bases	4	1	Self
	Batting Average	9	2	Self
1916	Runs Scored	5	10	Babe Ruth
	Stolen Bases	5	1	Self
1917	Hits	7	2	Self
	Singles	6	2	Self
	Total Bases	6		Tied by Babe Ruth and Ted Williams
	Stolen Bases	6	45	Luis Aparicio

	Batting Average	10	1	Self
	Slugging Average	8	10	Babe Ruth
1918	Batting Average	11	1	Self
1919	Hits	8		**Never broken**
	Singles	7	40	Nellie Fox
	Batting Average	12		**Never broken**

Season Fielding Records-CF

1911	Putouts	376	1	Burt Shotton
	Total Chances	418	1	Burt Shotton

Career Batting Records 1905-28

	Games Played	3,034	55	Carl Yastrzemski
	At Bats	11,429	55	Carl Yastrzemski
	Hits	4,191		**Never broken**
	Singles	3,052		**Never broken**
	Triples	297		**Never broken**
	Home Runs	118	1	Ken Williams
	Extra Base Hits	1,139	6	Babe Ruth
	Total Bases	5,863		**Never broken**
	Runs Scored	2,245		**Never broken**
	Batting Average	.367		**Never broken**
	RBIs	1961	6	Babe Ruth
	Stolen Bases	892	64	Rickey Henderson

Career Fielding Records-CF 1905-26

	Games Played	2,666	2	Tris Speaker
	Putouts	5,207	2	Tris Speaker
	Assists	293	2	Tris Speaker
	Double Plays	80	2	Tris Speaker
	Errors	214	2	Tris Speaker
	Total Chances	5,714	2	Tris Speaker

Career Batting Title Records 1905-26

	Hits Titles	8		**Never broken**
	Singles Titles	7	40	Nellie Fox
	Runs Scored Titles	5	10	Babe Ruth
	RBI Titles	4	15	Babe Ruth

Stolen Base Titles	6	45	Luis Aparicio
Batting Average Titles	1.2		**Never broken**
Slugging Average Titles	8	10	Babe Ruth

Major League Records

Season Batting Records

1911	Hits	248	9	George Sisler
	Stolen Bases	83	1	Clyde Milan
1915	Stolen Bases	96	47	Maury Wills

Season Batting Title Records

1909	Triple Crown	1	16	Rogers Hornsby
1911	MVP Title	1	13	Walter Johnson
	Hits Titles	4	1	Self
	RBI Titles	4	15	Babe Ruth
1912	Hits Titles	5	3	Self
	Singles Titles	4	3	Self
1914	Batting Average Titles	8	1	Self
	Slugging Average Titles	7	3	Self
1915	Hits Titles	6	2	Self
	Singles Titles	5	2	Self
	Batting Average Titles	9	2	Self
	Total Base Titles	5	2	Self
	Runs Scored Titles	4	1	Self
1916	Runs Scored Titles	5	10	Babe Ruth
1917	Hits Titles	7	2	Self
	Singles Titles	6	2	Self
	Total Base Titles	6	12	Rogers Hornsby
	Batting Average Titles	10	1	Self
	Slugging Average Titles	8	10	Babe Ruth
1918	Batting Average Titles	11	1	Self
1919	Hits Titles	8		**Never broken**
	Singles Titles	7	40	Nellie Fox
	Batting Average Titles	12		**Never broken**

Career Batting Records 1905-26

Games Played	3,034	48	Hank Aaron
At Bats	11,429	48	Hank Aaron
Hits	4,191	56	Pete Rose

Singles	3,052	56	Pete Rose
Runs Scored	2,245		**Never broken**
RBIs	1,961	7	Babe Ruth
Extra Base Hits	1,139	7	Babe Ruth
Total Bases	5,863	35	Stan Musial
Stolen Bases	892	51	Lou Brock
Batting Average	.367		**Never broken**

Career Batting Title Records 1905-26

Hits Titles	8		**Never broken**
Singles Titles	7	40	Nellie Fox
Total Base Titles	6	12	Rogers Hornsby
Runs Titles	5	10	Babe Ruth
RBI Titles	4	15	Babe Ruth
Batting Average Titles	12		**Never broken**
Slugging Average Titles	8	10	Babe Ruth

Career Fielding Records-CF 1905-26

Games Played	2,666	2	Tris Speaker
Putouts	5,207	2	Tris Speaker
Assists	293	2	Tris Speaker
Errors	214	2	Tris Speaker
Double Plays	80	2	Tris Speaker
Total Chances	5,714	2	Tris Speaker

World Series Records

Game Batting Records

1908	Stolen Bases	2	1	Honus Wagner
	Hits	4	74	Paul Molitar

Game Fielding Records-RF

1907	Putouts	5	5	Red Murray
1908	Errors	1	9	Eddie Collins
1909	Errors	1	8	Eddie Collins

5-Game Series Batting Records

1907	Triples	1	6	Eddie Collins

5-Game Series Fielding Records-RF

1907	Putouts	10	6	Eddie Murphy
	Errors	1	14	Ross Youngs

7-Game Series Fielding Records-RF

1909	Putouts	8	11	Tommy Griffith
	Errors	1	55	Mickey Mantle

Career Batting Records 1905-28

	Games Played	17	1	Wilfire Schulte
	Hits	17	1	Wilfire Schulte
	Singles	12	1	Frank Chance
	Series Played	3	1	Harry Steinfeldt & Wilfire Schulte

Career Fielding Records-RF 1905-28

	Putouts	21	9	Harry Hooper
	Errors	2	15	Ross Youngs
	Series Played	3	1	Harry Steinfeldt & Wilfire Schulte

Summary

Ty Cobb did not break any of Babe Ruth's records because he retired before the Babe. But his record profile is necessary so that comparisons can be made between two of the game's greatest players. The thing to note is the number of Ty Cobb's records Babe Ruth was successful in breaking. In 1921, Ruth broke the first of Cobb's records when he drove in more runs in one season. In that year, Ruth also won his fifth RBI title, breaking Cobb's record of four titles. In 1926, Ruth captured his sixth runs scored title and surged ahead of Cobb in this department.

In total base titles, Cobb was tied by the Babe and also Ted Williams. By 1917, Cobb had won his eighth slugging title, which comes as a surprise to many baseball experts. Cobb was considered a slap hitter, yet this record clearly shows that his slugging average was superior to the players of his era. It would take Babe Ruth to win more slugging titles than the Georgia Peach.

When Cobb retired in 1928, he had connected for more extra base hits than any player in the game. This record he also surrendered to Ruth in 1934. Also in 1934, the mighty Bambino passed Cobb in the RBI category. But there were also some records that even Babe Ruth could not' break. Ruth could not come close to the lifetime batting average of Ty Cobb. Nor could any other player in baseball. Cobb won the most hits titles 8 times and batting average title 12 times; These records have never been broken. Also never broken is the 2,245 runs scored record by Cobb.

Other great players who have broken Ty Cobb's records are: Eddie Collins, Rickey Henderson, Ted Williams, Nellie Fox, Burt Shotton, Carl Yastrzemski, Tris Speaker, Luis Aparicio, George Sisler, Maury Wills, Rogers Hornsby, Hank Aaron, Stan Musial, Lou Brock, Honus Wagner, Paul Molitar, Ross Youngs, and Pete Rose.

Ty Cobb played baseball with exceptional intensity. He hated to lose and was one of the most feared base runners the game had ever known. He did whatever it took to win, including sliding into bases with spikes flying high. He openly declared that the base paths were his.

Prior to Babe Ruth, Cobb was the greatest player in baseball. Some think he still is and will always be. He led the American League in various batting departments a phenomenal 52 times! Seven times he belted more than 200 hits in a season. He was also an excellent defensive player, who led the league in fielding eight times.

Most amazing is that Ty put his spikes on for 24 years and batted well over .300 for 23 consecutive years! This feat has never been approached by any player in baseball history. He became a Hall of Famer in 1936.

Postseason Awards

1909   Triple Crown
1911   MVP

Career statistics

Years: 24
Strikeouts: 357
Home Run %: 1.0
At Bats 11,429: (4th)
Slugging Average: .513
RBIs: 1,961 (4th)
Doubles: 724 (4th)
Pinch Hits: 15
Stolen Bases: 892 (3rd)

Home Runs: 118
Games: 3,034 (4th)
Batting Average: .367 (1st).
Runs: 2,245 (1st.)
Hits: 4,191 (2nd)
Pinch Hit at Bats: 69
Walks: 1,249
Triples: 297 (2nd)

Quotes From Ty Cobb

"The baseline belongs to me."

"I just got to be first – all the time."

"Every great batter works on the theory that the pitcher is more afraid of him than he is of the pitcher."

"I observed that baseball is not unlike a war, and we batters are the heavy artillery."

RECORD PROFILE

HENRY LOUIS GEHRIG

b. June 19, 1903, d. June 6, 1941
(The Iron Horse, The Pride of the Yankees, Lou,
Twinkle Toes, Columbia Lou)
NY-AL, 1923-39

Number of Records Established-53

American League Records

	Years lasted before broken		Broken by:
Rookie Batting Records			
1925 Most Home Runs	20	4	Dale Alexander
Season Batting Records			
1927 RBIs	175	4	Self
1931 RBIs	184		**Never broken**
Season Batting Title Records			
1934 Triple Crown	1	13	Ted Williams
1936 MVP Titles	2	2	Jimmie Foxx
Season Fielding Records-1B			
1938 Double Plays	157	6	Rudy York

Career Batting Records 1923-39

Cons. Games Played	2,130		**Never broken**
Grand Slams	23		**Never broken**

Career Records-1B 1923-39

Games Played	2,136	19	Mickey Vernon
Cons. Games Played	2,130		**Never broken**
Putouts	19, 510	19	Mickey Vernon
Double Plays	1,574	8	Joe Kuhel
Total Chances	20,790	19	Mickey Vernon

Major League Records

Season Batting Records

1927 RBIs	175	3	Hack Wilson

Season Batting Title Records

1936 MVP Titles	2	2	Jimmie Foxx

Season Fielding Records-1B

1938 Double Plays	157	6	Rudy York

Career Batting Records 1923-39

Cons. Games Played	2,130		**Never broken**
Grand Slams	23		**Never broken**

Career Fielding Records-1B 1923-39

Cons. Games Played	2 ,130		**Never broken**

All-Star Game Records

Game Batting Records

1933	Games Played	1	1	Tied by many
	Bases On Balls	2	1	Charlie Gehringer
1934	Games Played	2	1	Tied by many
1935	Game s Played	3	1	Tied by many
1936	Games Played	4	1	Tied by Ben Chapman, Gabby Hartnett, and Charlie Gehringer
	Home Runs	1	5	Arky Vaughn
1937	Games Played	5	1	Gabby Hartnett and Charlie Gehringer

Home Runs	1	4	Arky Vaughn
Total Bases	6	4	Arky Vaughn
Extra Base Hits	2		Tied by many
RBIs	4	9	Ted Williams
1938 Games Played	6	4	Arky Vaughn

Game Fielding Records-1B

1933 Putouts	12	15	George McQuinn
1935 Putouts	12	13	George McQuinn

Career Batting Records 1923-39

Games Played	6	4	Arky Vaughn
Runs	4	4	Arky Vaughn
RBIs	5	12	Joe DiMaggio
Home Runs	2	22	Ted Williams
Extra Base Hits	3	22	Ted Williams
Strikeouts	6	3	Jimmie Foxx

Career Fielding Records-1B 1923-39

Putouts	54		**Never broken**
Errors	2	24	Stan Musial

World Series Records

4-Game Series Batting Records

1927 Triples	2		Tied by Tommy Davis
1928 Bases on Balls	6	26	Hank Thompson
Home Runs	4		**Never broken**
RBIs	9		**Never broken**
Slugging Average	.727	11	Charlie Keller
1932 Runs Scored	9		Tied Babe Ruth

4-Game Series Fielding Records-1B

1927 Assists	3	26	Vic Wertz
1932 Errors	1		Tied by Vic Wertz
1938 Assists	3	16	Vic Wertz

Career Batting Records 1923-39

RBIs	35	25	Yogi Berra

Career Fielding Records-1B 1923-39

Putouts	309	21	Gil Hodges
Total Chances	321	21	Gil Hodges

Summary

One record that may never be broken is Lou Gehrig's 2,130 consecutive games played. He did not miss a game in 14 years. He seemed indestructible and his illness was a shock that was long mourned by the baseball world.

He played in the shadow of Babe Ruth, yet more than held his own. He was called, "The Pride of the Yankees," and he was that and more. During his fabulous 17-year career, the solidly built lefty batted over .300 fourteen times. He enjoyed his highest batting average in 1930 when he terrorizied opposing pitchers with a hefty .379. Only 14 players have a lifetime batting average above Lou's .340 and his slugging average of .632 has only been topped by Babe Ruth and Ted Williams. He broke more of Babe Ruth's records than any player in baseball history (9).

Gehrig won the MVP award in 1927 when he batted .373, had 52 doubles, 47 homers and 175 RBIs. He won the Triple Crown in 1934 with 49 homers, 165 RBIs and a .363 batting average. In 1936 he won his second MVP honor by smashing 205 hits, 49 homers and 152 RBIs while slugging a smart .696 and batting .354. Only two players in the history of the game have driven in more runs (Ruth and Aaron). This was truly remarkable when one considers that from 1925 to 1934 Babe Ruth cleared the bases 424 times with home runs. The question asked is, "How many more RBIs would Gehrig have if he batted before the Babe in the Yankee line-up?"

Postseason Awards

1927 MVP	1936 MVP
1934 Triple Crown	1939 Hall of Fame

Career Statistics

Years: 17

Strikeouts: 789

Home Run %: 6.2

At Bats: 8,001

Slugging Ave.: .632 (3rd)

RBIs: 1990 (3rd)

Doubles: 535

Pinch Hits: 4

Stolen Bases: 102

Home Runs: 493

Games: 2,164

Batting Average: .340

Runs: 1888 (7th)

Hits: 2,712

Pinch Hit At Bats: 16

Walks: 1508 (10th)

Triples: 162

Quotes From Lou Gehrig

"The ballplayer who loses his he head, who can't keep cool, is worse than no ballplayer at all."

"Joe, I'm out of the lineup. I'm just not doing the team any good." (to manager Joe McCarty after playing 2,130 games).

"Fans, for the past two weeks you have been reading about what a bad break I got. Yet today I consider myself the luckiest man on the face of the earth. I might have had a tough break, but I have an awful lot to live for." (His farewell speech.)

Quotes About Lou Gehrig

"Lou was the kind of boy that if you had a son he's the kind of person you'd like your son to be." (Sam Jones, teammate.)

"Gehrig never learned that a ballplayer couldn't be good every day." (Hank Gowdy, Braves catcher.)

RECORD PROFILE

Joseph Paul DiMaggio

(The Yankee Clipper, Joltin' Joe)
b. Nov. 25, 1914
NY-AL 1936-51

Number of Records Established–26

American League Records

Rookie Batting Records	Years lasted before broken	Broken by:
1936 Most Runs Scored	132	**Never broken**
Rookie Fielding Records-LF		
1936 Highest Fielding Average	.978 43	Billy Sample
Season Batting Records		
1941 Longest Hitting Streak	56	**Never broken**
Season Fielding Records-CF		
1947 Highest Fielding Average	.997 21	Mickey Stanley
Career Batting Title Record 1936-51		
Most MVP Titles	3	Tied Jimmie Foxx; tied by Yogi Berra, & Mickey Mantle

Major League Records

Season Batting Records

1941	Longest Hitting Streak	56		**Never broken**

Season Fielding Records-CF

1947	Highest Fielding Average	.997	5	Tony Gonzalez

Career Batting Titles Records 1936-51

	Most MVP Titles	3	Tied Jimmie Foxx Tied by Stan Musial, Roy Campanella, Yogi Berra & Mickey Mantle

All-Star Game Records

Game Batting Records

1939	Home Runs	1	2	Arky Vaughn
1941	Runs Scored	3	5	Ted Williams
1950	Games Played	11	13	Stan Musial

Career Batting Records 1936-51

	Games Played	11	13	Stan Musial
	At Bats	40	13	Stan Musial
	RBIs	6	10	Ted Williams
	Runs	7	10	Ted Williams

World Series Records

Game Batting Records

1936	At Bats	6	37	Don Hahn

5-Game Series Fielding Records-CF

1937	Putouts	18	5	Self
1942	Putouts	20		**Never broken**

6-Game Fielding Records-CF

1936	Putouts	18	8	Mike Kreevich
	Errors	1		Tied by many

Career Batting Records 1936-51

	Games Played	51	4	Phil Rizzuto
	At Bats	199	13	Yogi Berra
	Series Played	10	13	Yogi Berra

Career Fielding Records-CF 1936-51

Putouts	150	**Never broken**
Total Chances	151	**Never broken**
Chances w/o Errors	132	**Never broken**

Summary

"Joltin' Joe's" 56-game hitting streak remains one of baseball's greatest treasures. Since 1941, only Pete Rose has made a serious attempt at it, but came up short with 44.

The "Yankee Clipper" ran up 26 outstanding records, 12 of which still stand today. He was a league leader in various batting departments 11 times, and his lifetime slugging average of .579 is the sixth best in baseball. This is a tremendous accomplishment since he played most of his games in Yankee stadium, where "death valley" took away many extra base hits and would be home runs in most other ball parks.

DiMaggio batted over .300 in eleven of the thirteen seasons he wore the Yankee pinstripes. He probably would have added another three had he not lost three years serving his country in World War II.

During World Series play, he compiled 11 outstanding records. His 199 at bats is the third best; he ranks fourth in hits, fifth in runs scored and RBIs, and seventh in games played and home runs.

Joe was also super in All-Star games where he added another seven records. At the time of his retirement he had played in more All-Star games, had more at bats, scored more runs, and had more RBIs than any player in All-Star game history.

Despite the fact that most of DiMaggio's 400-foot fly balls would have been home runs in most other stadiums, he still has the best ratio of home runs to strikeouts than any player in the game. DiMaggio hit 361 home runs and only struck out 369 times.

Joe DiMaggio was inducted into the Hall of Fame in 1955.

Postseason Awards

1939 MVP
1941 MVP
1947 MVP

Career Statistics

Years: 13
Strikeouts: 369
Home Run %: 5.3
At Bats: 6,821
Slugging Average: .579
RBIs: 1,537
Doubles: 389
Pinch Hits: 6
Stolen Bases: 30

Home Runs: 361
Games: 1,736
Batting Average: .325
Runs Scored: 1,390
Hits: 2,214
Pinch Hit At Bats: 12
Walks: 790
Triples: 131

Quotes From Joe DiMaggio

"I'd like to thank the good Lord for making me a Yankee."

"There's always some kid who may be seeing me play for the first time. I owe him my best." (When asked why he played so hard.)

"I can remember a reporter asking for a quote, and I didn't know what a quote was. I thought it was some kind of a soft drink."

"A ballplayer's got to be kept hungry to become a big leaguer. That's why no boy from a rich family ever made the big leagues."

"I no longer have it, and when baseball is no longer fun, it is no longer a game." (about his retirement.)

RECORD PROFILE

STANLEY FRANK MUSIAL

(Stan the Man)
b. Nov. 21, 1920
St. Louis-NL 1941 - 63

Number of Records Established-53

National League Records

Season Batting Records		Years lasted before broken		Broken by:
1946	Most MVP Titles	2	2	Self
1948	Most MVP Titles	3		Tied by Roy Campanella
	Most Hits Titles	4	1	Self
	Most Triples Titles	3	1	Self
1949	Most Hits Titles	5	3	Self
	Most Triples Titles	4	2	Self
1951	Most Triples Titles	5		**Never broken**
1952	Most Hits Titles	6	29	Pete Rose
1954	Most Doubles Titles	8		Tied Honus Wagner
	Most Runs Scored Titles	5		Tied George Burns and Rogers Hornsby

Career Batting Records 1941-63

Games Played	3,026	11	Hank Aaron
At Bats	10,972	11	Hank Aaron
Hits	3,630	23	Pete Rose
Doubles	725	23	Pete Rose
Extra Base Hits	1,377	11	Hank Aaron
Total Bases	6,134	11	Hank Aaron
Runs Scored	1,949	10	Willie Mays
RBIs	1,951	11	Hank Aaron

Career Batting Title Records 1941-63

Most MVP Titles	3		Tied Jimmie Foxx, Joe DiMaggio, Roy Campanella, Yogi Berra; tied by Mickey Mantle
Most Hits Titles	6	5	Pete Rose
Most Doubles Titles	8		Tied Honus Wagner
Most Triples Titles	5		**Never broken**
Most Runs Scored Titles	5		Tied George Burns and Rogers Hornsby

Major League Records

Season Batting Title Records

1948	Most MVP Titles	3		Tied Jimmie Foxx, Joe DiMaggio, Roy Campanella, Yogi Berra; tied by Mickey Mantle
1954	Most Doubles Titles	8		Tied Honus Wagner and Tris Speaker
1951	Most Triples Titles	5		Tied Sam Crawford

Career Batting Records 1941-63

Extra Base Hits	1,377	13	Hank Aaron
Total Bases	6,134	13	Hank Aaron

Career Batting Title Records 1941-63

Doubles Titles	8		Tied Honus Wagner and Tris Speaker
Triples Titles	5		Tied Sam Crawford

All-Star Game Records

Game Batting Records

1954	Games	11	1	Self
1955	Games	12	1	Self
1956	Games	13	1	Self
1957	Games	14	1	Self
1958	Games	15	1	Self
1959	Games	16	1	Self
1959	Games	17	1	Self
1960	Games	18	1	Self
1960	Games	19	1	Self
1961	Games	20	1	Sell
1961	Games	21	1	Self
1962	Games	22	1	Self
1962	Games	23	1	Self
1963	Games	24		Tied by Willie Mays

Fielding Records-1B

1958 Double Plays	3		Tied by Bill White

Career Batting Records 1941-63

Games	24		Tied by Willie Mays
At Bats	63	10	Willie Mays
Hits	20	10	Willie Mays
Runs Scored	10	10	Willie Mays
Home Runs	6		**Never broken**
Total Bases	40		**Never broken**
Extra Base Hits	8		Tied by Willie Mays

World Series Records

5-Game Series Fielding Records-RF

1943 Assists	2		Tied by many

Summary

Stan "The Man" Musial batted over .300 in 18 of his 22 years in baseball. He led the National League in various batting categories a remarkable 40 times!

Stan won the most hits crowns four times and was an eight-times doubles king and a five-times triples leader; he led in runs scored five times, RBIs twice, bases on balls once, was a batting average leader seven times and led the league in slugging six times! These are phenomenal feats accomplished for the difficult pitching of modern baseball, which threw tough left-handed relief pitching at "The Man" in attempts to get him out. Even with their blazing 90-miles-an-hour fast balls, split-fingered fast balls, and wicked sliders, pitchers found it extremely difficult in getting Musial out.

On the all-time batting lists, Musial ranks third in doubles, fourth in hits, fifth in games played, at bats, and RBIs, sixth in runs scored, eighth in bases on balls, and ninth in slugging average. He is ranked in the top ten of all baseball greats.

On defense, he played right field, left field, and first base, and he did very well wherever he was asked to play. Eight times he led the league in various fielding categories.

Musial is one of the rare major-leaguers who have won the MVP award three times. Stan compiled 53 outstanding records, one of which took the extra base hits record away from Babe Ruth. Eighteen times he broke his own record; 16 of his records have been tied, 4 remain unbroken, and 15 times his records have been broken by others.

Musial's talents simply could not be overlooked. In his 22-year career, he was voted to the All-Star team a record 24 times. Only Willie Mays has been able to tie this marvelous record. When Musial retired, he had played in more All-Star games, had more at bats, hits, home runs, total bases, extra base hits, and scored more runs than any player in the history of baseball. He is still the leader in home runs and total bases and has been tied by Willie Mays in two departments. May has broken three of Musial's All-Star game records. "The Man" entered the Hall of Fame in 1969.

Postseason Awards

MVP 1943, 1946 and 1948

Career Statistics

Years: 22

Strikeouts: 696

Home Run %: 4.3

At Bats: 10,972

Slugging Average: .559

RBIs: 1,951

Double:s 725

Pinch Hits: 35

Stolen Bases: 78

Home Runs: 475

Games: 3,026

Batting Average: .331

Runs Scored: 1,949

Hits: 3,630

Pinch Hit At Bats: 126

Walks: 1,599

Triples: 177

RECORD PROFILE

ROGERS HORNSBY
(The Rajah)

b. Apr. 27, 1896, d. Jan. 5, 1963

StL-NL 1915-26, NY-NL 1927, Bos-NL 1928, Chi-NL
1929-32, StL-NL 1933, StL-AL 1933-37

Manager: StL-NL 1925-26, Bos-NL 1928, Chi-NL 1930-32,
StL-AL 1933-37, 1952, Cin-NL 1952-53

Number of Records Established-41

National League Records

Season Batting Records	Years lasted before broken		Broken by:
1921 Total Bases	378	1	Self
1922 Total Bases	450		**Never broken**
Hits	250	7	Lefty O'Doul
Home Runs	42	7	Chuck Klein
Home Run %	6.7	1	Cy Williams
Extra Base Hits	102	8	Chuck Klein
Slugging Average	.722	3	Self
1925 Home Run %	7.7	5	Hack Wilson
Slugging Average	.756		**Never broken**

Season Batting Title Records

1922	Triple Crown	1	3	Self
1924	Hits Titles	4	25	Stan Musial
	Total Base Titles	5	1	Self
	Slugging Average Titles	6	1	Self
1925	MVP Titles	1	4	Self
	Triple Crown Titles	2		Tied by Ted Williams
	Total Base Titles	6	4	Self
	RBI Titles	4		Tied by Hank Aaron and Mike Schmidt
	Slugging Average Titles	7	3	Self
1928	Slugging Average Titles	8	1	Self
1929	MVP Titles	2	19	Stan Musial
	Total Base Titles	7	40	Hank Aaron
	Runs Scored Titles	5		Tied George Burns and tied by Stan Musial
	Slugging Average Titles	9		**Never broken**

Career Batting Records 1915-37

Home Runs	297	10	Mel Ott
Home Run %	3.7	10	Mel Ott
Slugging Average	.577		**Never broken**

Career Batting Title Records 1915-37

Triple Crown Titles	2		Tied by Ted Williams
MVP Titles	2	19	Stan Musial
Hits Titles	4	25	Stan Musial
Total Base Titles	7	40	Hank Aaron
Slugging Average Titles	9		**Never broken**
RBI Titles	4		Tied by Hank Aaron and Mike Schmidt
Runs Scored Titles	7		Tied George Burns and was tied by Stan Musial

Major League Records

Season Batting Title Records

1922	Triple Crown Titles	1	3	Self
1925	Triple Crown Titles	2		Tied by Ted Williams
	Total Base Titles	6	4	Self
	RBI Titles	4	1	Babe Ruth
	MVP Titles	1	4	Self
1929	MVP Titles	2	19	Stan Musial
	Total Base Titles	.	7 40	Hank Aaron

World Series Records

5-Game Series Batting Records

1929	Strikeouts	8	Tied by Duke Snider

Summary

One of the greatest National League players and right-handed hitters of all time was Rogers Hornsby. "The Rajah" was a league leader in various batting categories for a fabulous 43 times. He won the triple crown in 1922 and 1925 and was awarded the MVP title in 1925 and 1929. Proving that he was a great all-around player, Hornsby also won nine fielding titles as a second baseman.

Hornsby's achievements included seven seasons with more than 200 hits (four titles), seven seasons of more than 40 doubles (four titles), three seasons of 17 or more triples (two titles), five seasons of more than 25 home runs (two titles), three home run percentage crowns, six seasons of scoring more than 100 runs (five titles), five seasons of more than 100 RBIs (four titles), three bases on balls crowns, and 19 seasons of batting over .300. He never led the league in strikeouts. Four times he batted over .400 in a season (seven batting average titles). He had twelve seasons of slugging over .500, nine of which won him slugging titles. Hornsby is the only player in baseball history who had a 5-year batting average over .400. From 1921 through 1925 he averaged a phenomenal .402.

Hornsby played his career in the National League at almost the same time Babe Ruth played in the American League. Hornsby was to the National League what Babe Ruth was to the American League. In 1929 Hornsby won his seventh total base title, breaking the record of Babe Ruth. So great was this achievement that this new record would last 40 years before Hank Aaron would break it.

Hornsby was named to the Hall of Fame in 1942.

Postseason Awards

Triple Crown	1922
Triple Crown	1925
MVP	1925
MVP	1929

Career Statistics

Years: 23	Home Runs: 301
Strikeouts: 679	Games: 2,259
Home Run %: 3.7	Batting Ave.: .358 (end)
At Bats: 8,173	Runs Scored: 1,597
Slugging Ave.: .577 (7th)	Hits: 2,930
RBIs: 1,584	Pinch Hit At Bats: 86
Doubles: 541	Walks: 1,038
Pinch Hits: 26	Triples: 169
Stolen Bases: 135	

RECORD PROFILE

THEODORE SAMUEL WILLIAMS
(Toed, The Splendid Splinter, The Thumper)
b. Aug. 30, 1918
Bos-AL 1939-60
Manager: Was-AL 1969-70

Number of Records Estalished-26

American League Records

Rookie Batting Records	Years lasted before broken		Broken by:
1939 RBIs	145		**Never broken**
Bases on Balls	107		**Never broken**
Rookie Fielding Records-RF			
1939 Putouts	318	38	Jim Norris
Total Chances	348		**Never broken**
Season Batting Title Records			
1942 Triple Crown	1	5	Self
1947 Triple Crown	2		Tied Rogers Hornsby
1951 Total Base Titles	6		Tied Ty Cobb and Babe Ruth

Career Batting Title Records 1939-60

Triple Crown Titles	2		Tied Rogers Hornsby
Total Base Titles	6		Tied Ty Cobb and Babe Ruth

Major League Records

Rookie Batting Records

1939 RBIs	145	**Never broken**

World Series Records

7-Game Fielding Records-LF

1946 Assists	2	Tied by many

All-Star Game Records

Game Batting Records

1941 RBIs	4	5	Self
1946 RBIs	5		Tied By Al Rosen
Home Runs	2		Tied Arky Vaughn
Hits	4		Tied by Al Rosen, Willie McCovey, and Gary Carter
Runs Scored	4		**Never broken**
Extra Base Hits	2		Tied by many
Total Bases	10		**Never broken**
1951 Triples	1	27	Rod Carew
1957 At Bats	7		Tied Willie Jones

Career Batting Records 1939-60

Hits	14	3	Stan Musial
Runs Scored	10	13	Willie Mays
RBIs	12		**Never broken**
Home Runs	4	3	Stan Musial
Total Bases	30	3	Stan Musial
Extra Base Hits	7	3	Stan Musial
Bases on Balls	10		**Never broken**
Strikeouts	9	8	Mickey Mantle

Summary

Starring for the Boston Red Sox for 19 years, Ted Williams is considered by many to be the purest hitter in baseball history. He was the last of the modern players to hit over .400, a feat he accomplished in 1941, when he batted .406. Considering the tough relief pitching of his era, this was one of baseball's greatest achievements.

The "Splendid Splinter" led the American League in various batting departments an astonishing 43 times. He won back-to-back doubles crowns in 1948 and 1949 and did the same in home runs in 1941 and 1942. In all, Williams won four home run titles and four home run percentage crowns. He led the league six times in runs scored, including five times in a row from 1940 to 1947. "The Thumper" led in RBIs 4 times with a high of 159 in 1949.

With the eyes of an eagle, Williams refused to swing at balls out of the strike zone, and won bases on balls titles eight times in succession from 1941 to 1949. It was said that if Williams did not swing at a pitch, the umpires would automatically call the pitch a ball. Williams had the lowest ratio of strikeouts among sluggers, with more than 500 home runs. He won the batting average title six times and also won nine slugging average crowns. Most impressive about his accomplishments is that he possessed the highest on-base average of any player in baseball history.

When Williams won his sixth total base title in 1951, he tied two of the game's greatest players, Babe Ruth and Ty Cobb. Williams certainly belongs in their company. In 1942, Williams won his first triple crown and when he did it again in 1947 he became only the second player in baseball to achieve this feat; Rogers Hornsby had also won two triple crowns ln 1922 and 1925 in the National League. The great Red Sox slugger also won two MVP awards, the first coming in 1946 and the second in 1949.

Postseason Awards

1942 Triple Crown
1946 MVP
1947 Triple Crown
1949 MVP

Career Statistics

Years: 19
Strikeouts: 709
Home Run %: 6.8 (6th)
At Bats: 7,706
Average: .634 (2nd)
RBIs: 1,839 (10th)
Doubles: 525
Pinch Hits: 33
Stolen Bases: 24

Home Runs: 521 (8th)
Games: 2,292
Batting Average: .344 (6th)
Runs Scored: 1,798
Hits: 2,654
Pinch Hit at Bats: 111
Walks: 2,019 (2nd)
Triples: 71

RECORD PROFILE

JAMES EMORY FOXX

(Jimmie, Double X, The Beast)
b. Oct. 22, 1907, d. July 21, 1967
Phi-AL 1925-35, Bos-AL 1936-42, Chi-NL 1942-44,
Phil-NL 1945

Number of Records Established–13

American League Records

Season Batting Records	Years lasted before broken	Broken by:
1933 MVP Titles	2	Tied Walter Johnson
1938 MVP Titles	3	Tied by Joe DiMaggio, Yogi Berra and Mickey Mantle
Career Batting Title Records 1925-45		
MVP Titles	3	Tied by Joe DiMaggio, Yogi Berra and Mickey Mantle

Major League Records

Season Batting Title Records

1933 MVP Titles		2	Tied Walter Johnson
1938 MVP Titles		3	Tied by Joe DiMaggio, Yogi Berra, Mickey Mantle, Stan Musial and Roy Campanella

Career Batting Records 1925-45

MVP Titles		3	*Tied by the above*

All-Star Game Records

Game Batting Records

1935 Home Runs	1	6	Arky Vaughn
Total Bases	5	2	Lou Gehrig
RBIs	3	2	Lou Gehrig

Career Batting Records 1925-45

Games Played	7	2	Billy Herman
Strikeouts	7	19	Ted Williams

World Series Records

5-Game Series Batting Records

1929 Home Runs	2	40	Don Clendenon
Total Bases	14	40	Don Clendenon

Summary

When Jimmie Foxx won his second MVP title in 1933, he broke another of Babe Ruth's records, as well as breaking all the records of the others who had only won one MVP award. And "The Beast" didn't stop there. In 1938 he won his third MVP award, becoming the first man in baseball history to do so. Since then, Foxx has been tied by Joe DiMaggio, Yogi Berra, Mickey Mantle, Stan Musial, and Roy Campanella.

Jimmie Foxx was also known as "Double X." He was a frightening sight to enemy pitchers, with muscles protruding from everywhere. He led the league in home runs four times, and was the home run percentage king four times as well. He was a three-time RBI champion, twice a batting average king, and a five-time slugging average leader. He led the league in various batting departments a total of 26 times. Foxx was baseball's first player to win consecutive MVP awards in 1932 and 1933.

His lifetime slugging average of .609 is the fourth-best in baseball, and he also had a solid .325 batting average. Only six others have hit more home runs and only five others have driven in more runs. He became a Hall of Famer in 1951.

Postseason Awards

1932 MVP
1933 MVP
1938 MVP

Career Statistics

Years: 20
Strikeouts: 1,311
Home Run %: 6.6 (8th)
At Bats: 8,134
Average: .609 (4th)
RBIs: 1,921 (6th)
Doubles: 458
Pinch Hits: 30
Stolen Bases: 88

Home Runs: 534 (7th)
Games: 2,317
Batting Average: .325
Runs Scored: 1,751
Hits: 2,646
Pinch Hit At Bats: 112
Walks: 1,452
Triples: 125

RECORD PROFILE

CHARLES HERBERT KLEIN

(Chuck)
b. Oct. 7, 1904, d. Mar. 28, 1958
Phi-NL 1928-33, Chi-NL 1934-36, Phi-NL 1936-39,
Pit-NL 1939, Phil-NL 1940-44

Number of Records Established–8

National League Records

Season Batting Records	Years lasted before broken	Broken by:	
1929 Home Runs	43	1	Hack Wilson
1930 Doubles	59	2	Paul Waner
Extra Base Hits	107		**Never broken**
Season Fielding Records-RF			
1930 Total Chances	423	2	Babe Herman

Major League Records
Season Fielding Records-RF

1930 Total Chances	423	2	Babe Herman

All-Star Game Records

Game Batting Records

1933	Games Played	1		By many
1934	Games Played	2		By many

Career Batting Records 1928-44

Games Played	2		By many
Singles	2	1	Bill Terry

Summary

In 1930, Chuck Klein had the honor of breaking one of Babe Ruth's records. It was in the fielding department as a right fielder that Klein took the Babe's major league season total chances mark. In 1923, the mighty Babe had set a new record by turning in 409 total chances. Klein compiled 423 total chances in 1930.

Klein was a super player in his own right. He led the league 18 times in various batting categories. His lifetime batting average was a fine .320. He batted over .300 nine times and was a three-time slugging average champion, a four-time home run king, a three-time runs scored leader, and a two-time hits, doubles, and RBI leader. He was also an excellent defensive outfielder, who led the league six times in various fielding departments.

He won the MVP award in 1932 as a result of smashing 226 hits, 38 home runs, scoring 152 runs, driving in 137, batting .348 and slugging .646. In 1933, he won the triple crown with 28 home runs, 120 RBIs and a batting average of .368. He also slugged for a .602 average, scored 101 runs, and rapped 223 base hits.

Chuck Klein was inducted into the Hall of Fame in 1980.

Postseason Awards

1932 MVP
1933 Triple Crown

Career Statistics

Years: 17
Strikeouts: 521
Home Run %: 4.6
At Bats: 6,486
Slugging Ave.: .543
RBIs: 1,201
Doubles: 398
Pinch Hits: 28
Stolen Bases: 79

Home Runs: 300
Games: 1,753
Batting Average: .320
Runs Scored: 1,168
Hits: 2,076
Pinch Hit At Bats: 137
Walks: 601
Triples: 74

RECORD PROFILE

Floyd Caves Herman

(The Brooklyn Babe)
b. June 26, 1903
Bkn-NL 1926-31, Cin-NL 1932, Chi-NL 1933-34,
Pit-NL 1935, Cin-NL 1935-36, Det-AL 1937, Bkn-NL 1945

Number of Records Established-28

National League Records

		Years lasted before broken	Broken by:
Season Fielding Records-RF			
1932 Putouts	392	39	**Never broken**
Total Chances	424	45	Dave Parker

Major League Records
Season Fielding Records-RF

1932 Putouts	392	39	Del Unser
Total Chances	424	45	Dave Parker

Brooklyn Dodgers Club Records

Rookie Batting Records

1926	Extra Base Hits	57	3	Johnny Frederick
	Total Bases	248	3	Johnny Frederick
	Slugging Average	.500	2	Del Bissonette

Season Batting Records

1927	Pinch Hit At Bats	20	5	Johnny Frederick
	Pinch Hits	7	5	Johnny Frederick
1929	Total Bases	348	1	Self
	Batting Average	.381	1	Self
	Slugging Average	.612	1	Self
1930	Hits	241		**Never broken**
	RBIs	130	23	Roy Campanella
	Batting Average	.393		**Never broken**
	Slugging Average	.678		**Never broken**
	Home Runs	35	21	Gil Hodges
	Home Run %	5.7	11	Dolf Camilli
	Extra Base Hits	94		**Never broken**
	Total Bases	416		**Never broken**

Career Batting Records 1926-31

	Slugging Average	.552		**Never broken**

Career Fielding Records-RF 1926-31

	Most Years	7	2	Dixie Walker
	Total Chances game	1.9	2	Dixie Walker
	Fielding Average	.979	2	Dixie Walker

Cincinnati Reds Club Records

Season Batting Records

1932	Extra Base Hits	73	22	Ted Kluszewski

Season Fielding Records-RF

1932	Putouts	392	**Never broken**
	Total Chancesgame	2.9	Tied With Harry Heilmann
	Total Chances	424	**Never broken**

Summary

Not too many major league players can say, "I broke a record held by Babe Ruth." But this can be said by another "Babe," Babe Herman.

In 1932, Babe Herman; while playing right field for the Cincinnati Reds registered 392 putouts. This broke a record Babe Ruth had set in 1923 when he posted a season putout total of 378 . Herman's mark was a National League record which still stands today. It was also a major league record that would last 39 years before it was broken by Del User. Also in 1932, Herman registered 424 total chances, and that outstanding achievement lasted 45 years as National and Major League record before it was broken in 1977 by Dave Parker.

Babe Herman was an outstanding player who enjoyed a fine 13-year career in which he batted .324. He is one of a handful of players with a lifetime batting average over .320 who is not in the Hall of Fame.

Herman stood 6'4" and weighed a solid 190 pounds. He batted left and threw left. In nine of his thirteen years in the big leagues, Herman batted over .300. He started out as a rookie in 1926, batting .319 in 137 games. He established three Dodger rookie records with his 57 extra base hits, 248 total bases, and .500 slugging average. Herman was hit by the sophomore jinx in 1927 and only batted .272 in 1927, but he rebounded well in 1928 with a solid .340 batting average. In 1929, Herman set a new Dodger club record by tearing the cover off the ball at a fantastic .381 clip, and broke his own records for total bases and slugging average.

The "Brooklyn Babe" enjoyed his greatest season in 1930 when he batted a whopping .393, which no Dodger player has come close to in sixty-odd years. In his fantastic 1930 season, Herman posted eight Dodger club records, five of which have never been broken. Herman was traded to the Cincinnati Reds in 1932, but when he left the

Dodgers, he had compiled a six-year slugging average of .552, a record that still stands today.

The solid-hitting lefty right fielder did well with the Reds in 1932 as he belted 16 homers, 38 doubles, led the league in triples with 19, and batted a smart .326 while slugging a fine .541. Herman then spent two years with the Chicago Cubs and part of the 1935 season with the Pirates and the Reds. He then hit .300 again for the Reds in 1936, which would be his last full season. In 1937, he played 17 games with the Tigers and retired until 1945 when he suddenly appeared again with the Dodgers for 37 games.

In his 13 years in baseball, Herman came to bat 5,603 times and came away with 1,818 hits. He played in 1,552 games – which shows that he averaged more than one hit per game. That is the mark of an outstanding hitter, one that Hall of Fame voters should take into consideration.

Career Statistics

Years: 13
Strikeouts: 553
Run Percentage: 3.2
Runs Scored: 882
RBIs: 997
Walks: 520
Pinch Hit At Bats: 120
Walks: 520
Triples: 110

Home Runs: 181
Games: 1,552
Batting Average: .324
At Bats: 5,603
Slugging Average .532
Hits: 1,818
Doubles: 399
Pinch Hits: 32
Stolen Bases: 94

RECORD PROFILE

JOHN ROBERT MIZE
(The Big Cat)
b. Jan. 7, 1913
StL-NL 1936-41, NY-NL 1942-49, NY-AL 1949-53

Number of Records Established-24

National League Records

Rookie Batting Records	Years lasted before broken	Broken by:
1936 Highest Fielding Average	.994 2	Frank McCormick

World Series Records

4-Game Series Fielding Records-1B

1950 Most Assists	3 4	Vic Wertz

7-Game Series Batting Records

1952 Highest Slugging Average	1.106	Never broken

Career Batting Records 1936-53

Most Pinch Hits	3	Never broken

St. Louis Cardinals Club Records

Rookie Batting Records

1936	Most Home Runs	19	17	Ray Jablonski
	Pinch Hits	7	26	Fred Whitfield

Rookie Fielding Records-1B

1936	Fewest Errors	6		Never broken
	Fielding Average	.994		Never broken

Season Batting Records

1940	Most Home Runs	43		Never broken
	Games Played	154	22	Ken Boyer

Career Batting Records 1936-41

	Home Run %	5.8		Never broken
	Slugging Average	.605		Never broken

New York Giants Club Records

Season Batting Records

1947	Most Home Runs	51	18	Willie Mays
	Home Run %	8.7	8	Willie Mays

Season Fielding Records-1B

1947	Fewest Errors	6		Never broken
	Fielding Average	.996		Tied Bill Terry
1949	Fewest Errors	6		Never broken

Career Batting Records 1942-49

	Home Run %	6.2	31	Willie McCovey
	Slugging Average	.543	23	Willie Mays

Career Fielding Records-1B 1942-49

	Fielding Average	.993		Never broken

New York Yankee Club Records

Season Batting Records

1951	Most Pinch Hits	9	1	Self
1952	Most Pinch Hits	10	1	Self
	Pinch Hit At Bats	48	1	Self
1953	Most Pinch Hits	19		Never broken
	Pinch Hit At Bats	61		Never broken

Summary

Johnny Mize was voted into the Hall of Fame in 1981, 28 years after he retired from the game. The long wait for recognition was a great injustice to this outstanding player. Few realize that his lifetime slugging average of .562 was the eighth best in baseball . He was a rare player in that he was a slugger with an exceptional glove. His nickname, "The Big Cat," gave hints of his superior fielding talents, but few recognized him for the tremendous defensive player he was. Perhaps this was due to his ability in hitting the long ball. But Johnny Mize was truly a great all- round player.

His outstanding fielding talents should have been noticed right from his rookie season when he set a new fielding average record of .994 for National League first baseman. When he participated in the 1950 World Series with the New York Yankees, he established a new assists record for first basemen, and this was in the twilight of his career.

Mike began his career with the St. Louis Cardinals in 1936, and to this day no Cardinal rookie first baseman has had a higher fielding average or made fewer errors than he. When Mize was sent to the New York Giants, he tied the long-standing fielding average record of the great Bill Terry. The year was 1947 when he fielded .996 while making only six errors. He also committed only six errors in 1949, and no Giant first baseman has ever done better.

But Johnny Mize was also a splendid hitter, a rare slugger who was difficult to strike out. In 6,443 at bats, he only went down 524 times. He was at the end of his career in 1952 while a member of the New York Yankees, and he was obtained by them mainly to be used as a pinch hitter. But Mize was so valuable that in the 7-game World Series of 1952 he set a new slugging average record of 1.106, which has never been broken. In that series, Mize came to bat 15 times and connected for six hits, 3 of which were homers and one a double. To this day, no player has broken his World Series pinch hit record of three hits.

When Mize was a rookie with the Cardinals in 1936, he quickly displayed his hitting prowess by setting a Cardinal home run record blasting 19 balls out of the park. It would take 17 years before another Cardinal rookie would do better than Mize. He was even a great pinch hitter in his rookie season. Seven times he hit safely, and this record would stand for 26 years before being broken by Fred Whitfield.

An interesting trivia question is "Who is the Cardinal player who has hit the most home runs in one season?" Names that come to mind are: Stan Musial, Rogers Hornsby, Joe Medwick, and Enos Slaughter. But the answer is Johnny Mize. In 1940, "The Big Cat" put 43 balls in orbit and that record remains unbroken in, now, 52 years. Another trivia question could be, "What Cardinal player has the highest home run % and slugging average?" Not many would think of Johnny Mize, but he is the man with these fabulous records.

Mike was just as successful while a member of the New York Giants. He set a new home run record in 1947, when be hit 51 and had a home run percentage of 8.7. Only the great Willie Mays could do better. And in the fielding average department, no Giant first baseman has been able to break Mize's average of .993 as a career record.

Johnny Mize was not only a club leader, but a National League leader as well. Four times he led the league in slugging average, winning the crowns three times in succession from 1938 to 1940. Four times he led the league in home runs and three times he was the RBI leader. In all, Mize led the league in various batting departments 20 times. Nine times he batted over .300, which he did consecutively. When he was sent to the Yankees, he led the league in pinch hitting for three years in a row.

Career Statistics

Years: 15
Strikeouts: 524
Home Run %: 5.6
At Bats: 6,443
Slugging Average: .562
RBIs: 1,337
Doubles: 367
Pinch Hits: 53
Stolen Bases: 28

Home Runs: 359
Games: 1,884
Batting Average: .312
Runs Scored: 1,118
Hits: 2,011
Pinch Hit at Bats: 187
Walks: 856
Triples: 83

RECORD PROFILE

Johnny Leonard Roosevelt Martin
(The Wild Hoss of the Osage, Pepper)
b. Feb. 29, 1904, d. Mar. 5, 1965
StL-NL 1928–44

Number of Records Established–17

All-Star Game Records

	Years lasted before broken		Broken by:
Game Batting Records			
1933 Games Played	1	1	Self & many
1934 Games Played	1	1	Self & many
1935 Games Played	1	1	Self & many
Stolen Bases	1	3	Charlie Gehringer
Career Batting Records 1928-44			
Games Played	3	1	Ben Chapman
Stolen Bases	1		Charlie Gehringer

World Series Records

Game Batting Records			
1931 Ibis	4	5	Bill Dickey
7-Game Series Batting Records			
1931 Hits	12	33	Bobby Richardson

Doubles	4	3	Pete Fox
Extra Base Hits	5	3	Pete Fox
Batting Average	.500		Tied by Johnny Lindell and Phil Garner
1934 Runs Scored	8		Tied Tommy Leach; tied by Billy Johnson Bobby Richardson, Mickey Mantle, and Lou Brock

7-Game Series Fielding Records-3B

1934 Most Errors		3 18	Gil McDougald

Career Batting Records 1928-44

Highest Batting Ave.	.418 (55/23)	**Never broken**

St. Louis Cardinals Club Records

Rookie Batting Records

1931 Most Doubles	32	2	Joe Medwick

Rookie Fielding Records-CF

1931 Fewest Errors	10	4	Terry Moore
Fielding Average	.967	4	Terry Moore

Summary

Some say the 1927 Yankees team was the greatest in baseball. But in St. Louis they would say that the 1934 team, which was affectionately called the "Gas House Gang," was not only the greatest, but the most colorful and picturesque.

Pepper Martin was a member of that team and he was frolicsome, exuberant, and possessed boundless energy. He was the type of player who would get right down into the dirt, and he played hard-nosed winning ball. Martin was known for his perspiration as well as his inspiration. On a hot day his nicely laundered uniform looked as out of place on him as a Lord Fauntleroy suit on a freckled Irish kid from St. Louis's old Kerry Patch.

The name "Gas House Gang" did not originate in St. Louis but was attributed to Leo Durocher. Dizzy Dean had remarked that the Cardinals could take up the lowly St. Louis Browns' winning percentage and still win the pennant in the American League. "They wouldn't let us play in that league," snapped Durocher, the former Yankee. "They'd say we were a lot of gas house ball players."

Pepper Martin didn't take long before the baseball world knew of his talents. As a rookie in 1931 he batted an even .300 and in 1933 was voted to the All-Star team. In that year he led the league in runs scored with 122 and stolen bases with 26 while batting .316. He also made the All-Star team in 1934 and 1935. Martin's name could easily come up in one of baseball's greatest trivia questions: "What player has the highest lifetime World Series batting average?" Not many would think of Pepper Martin, but the pesky little 5'8" 170-pounder came to bat 55 times and came away with 23 hits for a sensational .418 batting average. No player has ever done better.

Career Statistics

Years: 13

Strikeouts: 438

Home Run %: 1.4

At Bats: 4,117

Slugging Average: .443

RBIs: 501

Doubles: 270

Pinch Hits: 19

Stolen Bases: 146

Home Runs: 59

Games: 1,189

Batting Average: .298

Runs Scored: 756

Hits: 1,227

Pinch Hit at Bats: 91

Walks: 369

Triples: 75

RECORD PROFILE

JOSEPH EDWARD CRONIN

(Joe)
b. Oct. 12, 1906
Pit-NL 1926-27, Wash-AL 1928-34, Bos-AL 1935-45

Number of Records Established–28

All-Star Game Records

Game Batting Records	Years lasted before broken		Broken by:
1933 Games Played	1	1	Self & many
Runs Scored	1	1	Frankie Frisch
1934 Games Played	2	1	Self & many
1935 Games Played	3	1	Self & many
1936 Games Played	4	1	Self & many
1937 Games Played	5	1	Self & many
1939 Games Played	6	3	Arky Vaughn
Game Fielding Records-SS			
1933 Assists	4		Self
1934 Assists	8		**Never broken**
Career Batting Records 1926-45			
Games Played	6	3	Arky Vaughn

Doubles	3		Tied Al Simmons, was tied by Ted Kluszewski, Ernie Banks & Tony Oliva
Extra Base Hits	3	21	Ted Williams

Career Fielding Records-SS 1926-45

Most Assists	25		**Never broken**
Most Errors	1	1	Red Rolfe

Boston Red Sox Club Records

Season Batting Records

1939 Consecutive Games w/RBIs	12	3	Ted Williams
1943 Most Pinch Hits	18		**Never broken**

Season Fielding Records-SS

1938 Most Double Plays	110	7	Eddie Lake

Career Batting Records 1935-45

Most Doubles	270	6	Bobby Doerr
Pinch Hit At Bats	100	15	Gene Stephens
Pinch Hits	29	15	Ted Williams

Career Fielding Records-SS 1935-45

Most Years	8		Tied Everett Scott, and Heinie Wagner was tied by Rico Petrocelli
Most Double Plays	565	38	Rick Burleson

Manager's Records (Boston Red Sox)

Season Records

1947 Highest Finish	1st		Tied by many

Career Records 1935-47

Most Years	13		**Never broken**
Most Games	1,987		**Never broken**
Most Wins	1,071		**Never broken**
Most Losses	916		**Never broken**

World Series Games

Lost	4	Tied by Dick Williams, Darrell Johnson and John McNamara

Summary

Joe Cronin was a good-hitting shortstop with a lifetime batting average of .302, something that not many shortstops can claim. This covered a span of 20 years which showed that Cronin was consistently excellent. His best season was in 1930 when he batted .346 and belted 203 hits. Twice he was a league leader in doubles and rapped 515 two baggers during his wonderful career.

Not only could he hit but he was super with the glove as well. Sixteen times he was a league leader in various fielding departments.

Cronin was one of those rare players who doubled as a manager at the same time. He did this for the Washington Senators from 1933 to 1934 and for the Boston Red Sox from 1935 to 1945.

He was the first player to rise through the ranks to become president of either league. He was voted the outstanding shortstop by the *Sporting News* from 1930 to 1934 and in 1938 and 1939. In 1943, he set an American League record by hitting 5 pinch hit home runs.

Connie Mack was quoted as saying, "Joe Cronin was the best clutch hitter I ever saw."

From 1948 to 1959, Cronin served the Boston Red Sox as treasurer, vice president and general manager He became American League president in 1959 and held that position until 1973. He was the chairman of the American League board from 1973 to 1984 and was director of the National Baseball Hall of Fame. In 1970 he became chairman of its Veterans Committee and in 1977 became president of the Baseball Players Association. He helped incorporate the Reorganization Agreement into the American

League constitution and was instrumental in adding new teams to the league. He was voted into the Hall of Fame in 1956.

The All-Star games did not begin until 1933. Cronin was elected to the team as the best American League shortstop six times. Had the All-Star games started at an earlier date, Cronin would have been on the team three more times as he had brilliant seasons in 1929, 1930 and 1931. In the 1934 All-Star game, the slick fielding shortstop had 8 assists, a record which still stands today. During his All-Star career, he banged out 3 doubles and as of this writing this mark has only been tied. In his six All-Star games he had a total of 25 assists and this record has also never been broken.

When Cronin's career was reaching an end, he was used frequently as a pinch hitter. He enjoyed his best pinch hitting season in 1943, when he belted 5 home runs and had 18 hits. These records also remain unbroken.

Cronin also has four unbroken records as a Red Sox manager. He is the leader in most years, games, wins and losses of any Red Sox manager.

Career Statistics

Years: 20
Strikeouts: 700
Home Run %: 2.2
At Bats: 7,579
Slugging Average: .468
RBIs: 1,424
Doubles: 515
Pinch Hits: 30
Stolen Bases: 87

Home Runs: 170
Games: 2,124
Batting Average: .302
Runs Scored: 1,233
Hits: 2,285
Pinch Hit At Bats: 104
Walks: 1,059
Triples: 118

RECORD PROFILE

WILLIAM MALACOLM DICKEY
(Bill)
b. June 6, 1907
NY-AL 1928-46

Number of Records Established–28

American League Records

Season Fielding Records-Catcher	Years lasted before broken		Broken by:
1931 Highest Fielding Average	.996	15	Buddy Rosar
Career Fielding Records-Catcher 1928-46			
Most Putouts	7,965	19	Yogi Berra
Fielding Average	.988	5	Buddy Rosar

Major League Records

Season Fielding Records-Catcher

1931 Fielding Average	.996	1	Earl Grace
Career Fielding Records-Catcher 1928-46			
Most Putouts	7,965	19	Yogi Berra
Fielding Average	.988	5	Buddy Rosar

World Series Records

Game Batting Records

1932	Most At Bats	6 42	Don Hahn
1936	Most RBIs	5 22	Bobby Richardson
1938	Most Hits	4 44	Paul Molitar
	Most Singles	4 44	Paul Molitar

4-Game Series Fielding Records-Catcher

1938	Most Assists	5	Tied Gabby Hartnett

Career Fielding Records-Catcher 1928-46

Most Putouts	224	17	Yogi Berra
Total Chances	245	17	Yogi Berra
Chances w/o Errors	140	17	Yogi Berra

New York Yankee Club Records

Season Fielding Records-Catcher

1931	Putouts	670 2	Self
	Fewest Errors	3 27	Yogi Berra
	Total Chances	751 2	Self
	Fielding Average	.996 27	Yogi Berra
1933	Putouts	721 23	Yogi Berra
	Total Chances	809 31	Elston Howard

Rookie Fielding Records-Catcher

1929	Putouts	476 41	Thurmon Munson
	Total Chances	583 41	Thurmon Munson

Career Fielding Records-Catcher 1928-46

Putouts	7,965	17	Yogi Berra
Assists	942		**Never broken**
Fewest Errors per year	8.0	17	Yogi Berra
Double Plays	137	17	Yogi Berra
Total Chances	9,047	17	Yogi Berra
Fielding Average	.988	21	Elston Howard

Summary

Bill Dickey was one of baseball's finest all-round catchers. A lifetime batting average of .313 proved he could hit, and his 21 times of leading the league in fielding departments for catchers showed he was one of the best defensive men behind the plate.

The smooth swinging lefty batted over .300 eleven times with a high of .362 in 1936. In 1938, he set a World Series record by getting four hits in one game and in 1936 he drove in 5 runs in one World Series game, a mark that would last 22 years before Bobby Richardson would break it.

When his playing days were over he had a fabulous career as a coach and instructor. The Yankees needed a catcher to replace him. This player was Yogi Berra who was once called by Casey Stengel, " A funny looking man in a baseball suit." Yogi didn't have the body or the ambition of a successful catcher but Dickey's assignment was to make a catcher out of him. A quick look at who broke most of Dickeys catching records tells what a great job Dickey did with Yogi.

Career Statistics

Years: 17
Strikeouts: 289
Home Run %: 3.2
At Bats: 6,300
Slugging Average: .486
RBIs: 1,209
Doubles: 343
Pinch Hits: 18
Stolen Bases: 36

Home Runs: 202
Games: 1,789
Batting Average: .313
Runs Scored: 930
Hits: 1,969
Pinch Hit At Bats: 67
Walks: 678
Triples: 72

RECORD PROFILE

FRANK PETER JOSEPH CROSETTI
(The Crow)
b. Oct. 4, 1910
NY-AL 1932-48

Number of Records Established-13

American League Records

	Years lasted before broken		Broken by:
Season Fielding Records-SS			
1938 Most Double Plays	120	5	Lou Boudreau

World Series Records
Game Batting Records

1936 Most Runs Scored	4	Tied Babe Ruth, Earl Combs, and was tied by Reggie Jackson

New York Yankee Club Records
Season Fielding Records-SS

1938 Double Plays	120	12	Phil Rizzuto
Total Chances	905		**Never broken**

| 1939 | Fewest Errors | 26 | 8 | Phil Rizzuto |
| | Fielding Average | .968 | 8 | Phil Rizzuto |

Career Fielding Records-SS 1932-48

	Putouts	2,807		Never broken
	Assists	4,149		Never broken
	Errors	393		Never broken
	Fewest Errors			
	Per Year	30.0	6	Phil Rizzuto
	Double Plays	862		Never broken
	Total Chances	7,328		Never broken
	Most Years	17		Never broken

Summary

Frank Crosetti was only a .245 lifetime hitter but he enjoyed a marvelous baseball career. He had the honor of playing with Babe Ruth for three years, Lou Gehrig for eight years, and Joe DiMaggio for 13 years. He helped the Yankees win seven pennants and seven World Series. He then became a coach for the Yankees for the next 23 years. Frank Crosetti was truly a part of the Yankee dynasty. Always a gentleman, always a hustle and a familiar chirp that earned him the nick-name, "The Crow."

Crosetti placed some records in the Yankee book that will be very difficult to break. It will be a long, long time before another Yankee shortstop puts on the pin stripes for 17 years as Crosetti did. And along with that longevity comes the outstanding number of putouts, assists, errors, double plays and total chances that no other Yankee shortstop has come close to matching. Only Phil Rizzuto has been able to break the career fielding record of "The Crow."

Most players could only dream of breaking a record held by Babe Ruth. This ".250" hitter didn't quite break a Babe Ruth record, but he did manage to tie one. In the 1936 World Series, Crosetti scored four runs in one game. This tied a record that the Babe had set in 1926 and was subsequently tied by Earle Combs. Reggie Jackson was able to tie with Crosetti. But this remains an unbroken record that all of them can be proud of.

In all, "The Crow," placed 13 records in the book, seven have not been broken, one has been tied and Phil Rizzuto has taken over four of them and Lou Boudreau one other.

Career Statistics

Years: 17
Strikeouts: 801
Home Run %: 1.6
At Bats: 6,277
Slugging Average: .354
RBIs: 649
Doubles: 260
Pinch Hits: 7
Stolen Bases: 113

Home Runs: 98
Games: 1,682
Batting Average: .245
Runs Scored: 1,006
Hits: 1,541
Pinch Hit At Bats: 31
Walks: 792
Triples: 65

RECORD PROFILE

CHARLES LEONARD GEHRINGER

(Charlie)
b. May 11, 1903
Det-AL 1924-42

Number of Records Established–59

American League Records

	Years lasted before broken	Broken by:
Career Fielding Records-2B 1924-42		
Double Plays	1,444	9	Bobby Doerr
Fielding Average	.976	9	Bobby Doerr

Major League Records

Career Fielding Records-2B 1924-42			
Double Plays	1,444	9	Bobby Doerr
Fielding Average	.976	9	Bobby Doerr

All-Star Game Records

Game Batting Records			
1933 Games Played	1	1	Self & many
Runs Scored	1	1	Frank Frisch

1934	Games Played	2	1	Self & many
	Singles	2	3	Self
	Bases On Balls	3		Tied by Phil Cavaretta
1935	Games Played	3	1	Self and many
1936	Games Played	4	1	Self, Gabby Hartnett, and Lou Gehrig
1937	Games Played	5	1	Self, Lou Gehrig, and Joe Cronin
	Singles	3		Tied by Billy Herman, Bobby Avila, Ken Boyer, and Carl Yastremski
1938	Games Played	6	4	Arky Vaughn

Career Batting Records 1924-42

	Games Played	6	4	Arky Vaughn
	At Bats	29	12	Joe DiMaggio
	Hits	10	5	Billy Herman
	Singles	8	5	Billy Herman
	Total Bases	12	4	Arky Vaughn
	Bases On Balls	9	22	Ted Williams
	Stolen Bases	2	35	Willie Mays

Career Fielding Records-2B 1924-42

| | Assists | 15 | 1 | Billy Herman |

Detroit Tigers Club Records

Rookie Batting Records

| 1926 | Triples | 17 | | **Never broken** |

Rookie Fielding Records-2B

1926	Putouts	255	35	Jake Wood
	Fewest Errors	16	28	Frank Bolling
	Double Plays	56	35	Jake Wood
	Fielding Average	.973	28	Frank Bolling

Season Batting Records

| 1930 | Doubles | 47 | 4 | Hank Greenberg |
| 1936 | At Bats | 641 | 17 | Harvey Kuenn |

Season Fielding Records-2B

1926	Fewest Errors	16	9	Self
	Fielding Average	.973	3	Self
1927	Double Plays	84	1	Self
	Total Chances/Game	6.4		Tied by Gerry Priddy
1928	Assists	507	5	Self
	Double Plays	101	4	Self
	Total Chances	919	1	Self
1929	Total Chances	928	21	Gerry Priddy
	Fielding Ave.	.975	1	Self
1930	Fielding Ave.	.979	3	Self
1932	Double Plays	110	1	Self
1933	Assists	542	17	Tied by Gerry Priddy
	Double Plays	111	3	Self
	Fielding Ave.	.981	1	Self
1934	Fielding Ave.	.981	1	Self
1935	Fielding Ave.	.985	2	Self
	Fewest Errors	13	2	Self
1937	Fielding Ave.	.986	22	Frank Bolling
	Fewest Errors	12	4	Self
1941	Fewest Errors	11	18	Frank Bolling

Career Batting Records 1924-42

| | Home Runs | 184 | 4 | Hank Greenberg |
| | Bases On Balls | 1,185 | 32 | Al Kaline |

Career Fielding Records-2B 1924-42

	Most Years	19		Never broken
	Putouts	5,369		Never broken
	Assists	7,068		Never broken
	Errors	301		Never broken
	Double Plays	1,444		Never broken
	Total Chances/Game	5.7		Never broken
	Total Chances	12,738		Never broken
	Fielding Ave.	.976	17	Frank Bolling

Summary

Charlie Gehringer was one of baseball's greatest second basemen. During his 19-year career, he participated in more double plays and had the highest fielding average of any second baseman in baseball history. He was a league leader in various fielding categories 25 times.

He was truly a great all-round player who could hit as well as he could field. Charlie Gehringer retired with a lifetime batting average of .320 and led the league in various batting departments 9 times. His 574 doubles place him tenth on the all-time list.

Gehringer was a great player under pressure. When the competition was at the highest, such as in All-Star games and World Series, Gehringer was at his best. In three World Series, he belted 26 hits and batted a solid .321. In 6 All-Star games, he came to bat 29 times and had 10 hits for a .344 batting average.

The smooth fielding second baseman enjoyed his best season in 1937, when he batted .371, rapped 209 hits and won the MVP award. He was easily the greatest second baseman in Detroit history. A quick peek at his career fielding records show that no other Tiger second baseman has played as many years, had more putouts, assists, errors, double plays or total chances as he. Gehringer was elected into the Hall of Fame in 1949.

Postseason Awards   1937 MVP

Career Statistics

Years: 19

Strikeouts: 372

Home Run %: 2.1

At Bats: 8,860

Slugging Average: .480

RBIs: 1,427

Doubles: 574

Pinch Hits: 23

Stolen Bases: 182

Home Runs: 184

Games: 2,323

Batting Average: .320

Runs Scored: 1,774

Hits: 2,839

Pinch Hit At Bats: 91

Walks: 1,185

Triples: 146

RECORD PROFILE

WILLIAM BENJAMIN CHAPMAN

(Ben)
b. Dec. 25, 1908,
NY-AL 1930-36, Wash-AL 1936-37, Bos-AL 1937-38,
Cle-AL-1939-40, Wash-AL 1941, Chi-AL 1941, Bkn-NL
1944-45, Phil-NL 1945-46

Number of Records Established-12

All-Star Game Records

Game Batting Records	Years lasted before broken		Broken by:
1933 Games Played	1	1	Self & many
1934 Games Played	2	1	Self & many
1935 Games Played	3	1	Self & many
1936 Games Played	4	1	Gabby Hartnett, Charlie Gehringer and Lou Gehrig
1933 At Bats	5	16	Pee Wee Reese
1934 Triples	1	44	Rod Carew
Career Batting Records 1930-46			
Games Played	4	4	Gabby Hartnett, Charlie Gehringer and Lou Gehrig
Triples	1	37	Willie Mays

New York Yankee Club Records

Season Fielding Records

1933	Assists-LF	24	**Never broken**
1935	Assists-CF	25	**Never broken**
	Double Plays-CF	7	Tied Ray Demmitt and Earle Combs
	Total Chances/Game	3.0 9	Johnny Lindell

Summary

Ben Chapman was a .300 hitter, a blazing base stealer, and a difficult character. It was he, in 1934, who reportedly told an aging Babe Ruth, "If I were as old as you are, and as rich as you are, I wouldn't risk my health by playing anymore." There has never been a reported response to this from Babe Ruth.

Chapman burst onto the scene with his bat and mouth in 1930 and proved he could back up his bravado. He hit .316 as a rookie and then led the league three years in a row stealing 61, 38, and 27 bases while batting .315, .299 and .312. His best full season was in 1938, while a member of the Boston Red Sox, when he batted .340.

He was no Babe Ruth in the long ball department as the most home runs he could manage in one season was 17, back in 1931.

With the arrival of Joe DiMaggio, in 1936, Chapman was expendable as an outfielder and was traded off to the Washington Senators. He was a consistently good player who averaged 160 to 170 per season and ended his career with a solid .302 batting average.

Chapman could run like the wind and possessed a rifle arm. In 1933, he registered 24 assists from left field, and in 1935, he had 25 assists in center field. No Yankee player has ever broken these records. Also in 1935,

Chapman doubled up 7 runners and this record has only been tied by Ray Demmitt and Earle Combs.

Chapman was highly touted as a player and was voted to the All Star team four years in a row from 1933 to 1936. It was in this department that he broke a games played record held by Babe Ruth.

During the last 3 years of his career, Chapman turned to pitching because of his strong arm and while with the Dodgers in 1944, he won 5 and lost 3. He was 3 wins and 3 losses in 1945 and then ended his career with the Phillies in 1946 appearing in only one game.

Career Statistics

Years: 15

Strikeouts: 556

Home Run %: 1.4

At Bats: 6,478

Slugging Average: .440

RBIs: 977

Doubles: 407

Pinch Hits: 13

Stolen Bases: 287

Home Runs: 90

Games: 1,716

Batting Average: .302

Runs Scored: 1,144

Hits: 1,958

Pinch Hit At Bats: 43

Walks: 824

Triples: 107

RECORD PROFILE

Edwin Donald Snider

(Duke, The Silver Fox)
b. Sept. 19, 1926
Bkn-NL 1947-57, LA-NL 1958-62, NY-NL 1963, SF-NL 1964

Number of Records Established–8

National League Records

	Years lasted before broken	Broken by:
Career Batting Records 1947-64		
Strikeouts	1,237 3	Eddie Mathews

World Series Records

Game Fielding Records-CF		
1959 Errors	2 7	Willie Davis
5-Game Series Batting Records		
1949 Strikeouts	8	Tied Rogers Hornsby
7-Game Series Batting Records		
1952 Home Runs	4	Tied Babe Ruth
Extra Base Hits	6 27	Willie Stargell

Total Bases	24	27	Willie Stargell
RBIs	8	4	Mickey Mantle
1955 Home Runs	4		Tied Self and Babe Ruth and was tied by Hank Bauer and Gene Tenace

Career Batting Records 1947-64

Strikeouts	33	5	Mickey Mantle

Career Fielding Records-CF 1947-64

Errors	2	Tied by many

Brooklyn Dodgers Club Records

Season Batting Records

1953 Home Runs	42	3	Self
1955 Home Runs	42	1	Self
Home Run %	7.8		Self
1956 Home Runs	43		Never broken
Home Run %	7.9		Never broken
1957 Home Run %	7.9		Never broken
1962 Pinch Hit At Bats	33	12	Manny Mota

Career Batting Records 1947-62

Home Runs	389		Never broken
Home Run %	5.9		Never broken
Extra Base Hits	814		Never broken
RBIs	1,271		Never broken
Strikeouts	1,123		Never broken
Pinch Hit At Bats	147	20	Manny Mota
Pinch Hits	43	20	Manny Mota

Career Fielding Records-CF 1947-62

Years	16		Never broken
Putouts	2,750	11	Willie Davis
Total Chances	2,922	11	Willie Davis
Fielding Average	.987		Never broken

Summary

What can Duke Snider say he did better than Babe Ruth? In the seven game World Series of 1926, the mighty Babe blasted four home runs. Snider tied that record in 1952 and did a repeat performance in the 7 game series of 1955, thus becoming the first and only player in baseball history to accomplish this feat twice.

"The Duke," was the Dodgers most outstanding centerfielder and home run hitter. He was a complete player, excelling on defense as well as offense. A quick look at his Dodger career batting records reveals that of his 18 club records, 10 have never been broken and 3 were broken by himself. Snider did quite a bit of pinch hitting toward the end of his career and three of his pinch hitting records were broken by Manny Mota, the man who earned the reputation as one of baseball's greatest pinch hitters.

Willie Davis succeeded Snider in center field and was able to post more putouts and total chances to wrestle those marks away from Snider. However, Snider proved to have a steadier glove and no Dodger centerfielder has ever posted a higher lifetime fielding average.

Snider was one of baseball's most consistent hitters. During a five year span from 1953 to 1957, he belted the following number of home runs in each season: 42, 40, 42, 43, and 40. During that span his home run percentage was: 7.1, 6.8, 7.8, 7.9, and 7.9.

In an 18-year career, the great Dodger lefty blasted 407 homers and set 9 World Series marks. He led the league in various batting categories 11 times and won the runs scoring title three times in a row from 1953 to 1955. He also won titles in hits, RBIs, bases on balls, and was a two-time slugging average leader.

"The Duke" performed extremely well under the pressure of World Series play. He participated in six fall classics and clubbed 11 home runs, placing him fourth on the all-time list. He ranks fifth in home run percentage, sixth in doubles, seventh in RBIs, and tenth in runs scored. It is safe to say he was one of the all-time greats.

His talents were noticed by Hall of Fame voters in 1980.

Career Statistics

Years: 18
Strikeouts: 1,237
Home Run %: 5.7
At Bats: 7,161
Slugging Average: .540
RBIs: 1,333
Doubles: 358
Pinch Hits: 59
Stolen Bases: 99

Home Runs: 407
Games: 2,143
Batting Average: .295
Runs Scored: 1,259
Hits: 2,116
Pinch Hit At Bats: 223
Walks: 971
Triples: 85

RECORD PROFILE

CHARLES HERBERT RUFFING

(Red)

b. May 3, 1904

Bos-AL 1924-30, NY-AL 1930-46, Chi-AL 1947

NUMBER OF RECORDS ESTABLISHED-13

American League Records

	Years lasted before broken	Broken by:
Season Batting Records 1924-47		
Most Years Batting Over .300 by Pitcher	8	**Never broken**
Career Pitching Records 1924-47		
Most Bases on Balls	1,541 6	Bobo Newsom

All-Star Game Records

Game Pitching Records		
1934 Most Hits in one inning	4 20	Sandy Consequera
Career Pitching Records 1924-47		
Hits Allowed	13 15	Robin Roberts
Highest ERA	12.2 40	Goose Gossage

World Series Records

4-Game Series Pitching Records

1932	Bases On Balls	6 22	Bob Lemon
1938	Games Started	2	Tied by many
	Wins	2	Tied Dick Rudolph, Bill James and Waite Hoyt and was tied by Sandy Koufax
	Hits Allowed	17	**Never broken**

Career Pitching Records 1924–47

Wins	7 22	Whitey Ford
Strikeouts	61 9	Allie Reynolds
Series Played	7 22	Whitey Ford

Summary

In a fabulous 22-year career, "Red" Ruffing registered 273 wins and participated in seven World Series. He tossed 48 shutouts and was an eight-time league leader in various pitching departments.

Ruffling won 20 or more games for four consecutive seasons (1936-39) in leading the Yankees to four pennants.

"Red" was one of the best hitting pitchers in baseball history. He presently holds the record for most times hitting over .300 for pitchers. He accomplished this feat 8 times with a high batting average of .364, in 1930. He was often used as a pinch hitter and during his career belted 35 home runs which tie him for second place in this category.

Ruffing had one of the worst starts in baseball history. He began his career with the Boston Red Sox and in 135 games lost 96 and won only 39. Yet he went on to become a Hall of Famer.

After being traded to the Yankees in 1930, a flaw in his pitching delivery was straightened out by Yankee owner Ed Barrow, and the big redhead went on to win 226 games for the Yankees while losing only 114.

In World Series play, Ruffing's seven victories places him second on the all-time list. He became a Hall of Famer in 1967.

Career Statistics

Years: 22
Shutouts: 48
Games Completed: 335
Losses: 225
Relief Wins: 9
Hits: 4,294
ERA: 3.80
Saves: 16
Strikeouts: 1,987

Games Started: 536
Wins: 273
Relief Games: 88
Innings: 4,344
Winning Percentage: .548
Relief Losses: 15
Walks: 1,541
Total Games: 624

RECORD PROFILE

Charles Ernest Keller

(King Kong)
b. Sept. 12, 1916
NY-AL 1939-49, Det-AL 1950-51, NY-AL 1952

Number of Records Established–12

American League Records

		Years lasted before broken	Broken by:
Season Fielding Records-LF			
1943 Highest Fielding Average	.994	7	Hoot Evers

Ned York Yankee Club Records

Rookie Fielding Records-RF			
1939 Putouts	213		**Never broken**
Fewest Errors	7	28	Steve Whitaker
Total Chances / game	2.1		**Never broken**
Total Chances	225		**Never broken**
Season Fielding Records-LF			
1943 Highest Fielding Average	.994	28	Roy White
Fewest Errors	2	28	Roy White

Career Fielding Records-LF 1939-49

Highest Fielding Average	.980	5	Gene Woodling
Fewest Errors year	5.4	5	Gene Woodling
Total Chances / game	2.2		**Never broken**

World Series Records

4-Game World Series Batting Records

1939 Highest Slugging Average	1.188	**Never broken**

5-Game Series Batting Records

1942 Home Runs	2 27	Don Clendenon

Summary

In 1919, Babe Ruth played his first full season as an outfielder. In that year he led the league in fielding average posting a fantastic .992 fielding average while only committing 2 errors. This was truly remarkable for a player who had never played the outfield before. What was even more remarkable was that the Babe established this record with a glove that was not much bigger than his hand. The glove had no webbing and one wonders how any player of that era was able to hold onto a ball.

This would be the first and only fielding record Babe Ruth ever created. It is this record that Charlie Keller was able to take away from Babe Ruth. In 1943, with a much better glove, Keller also made only 2 errors, but because he had more chances, posted a record breaking .994 fielding average.

Charlie Keller became famous as part of a great Yankee outfield which had Joe DiMaggio in center field and Tommy Henrich in right. Keller, who was called "King Kong" because of his hairy muscular body, was instrumental in helping the Yankees win six pennants and five world series from 1939 through 1949.

Keller had great strength and took advantage of the right field wall in Yankee stadium and club and hammered 20 or more home runs for 5 of his first 7 years with the club.

He enjoyed three seasons with 30 or more home runs. He belted 33 in 1941, 31 in 1943 and 30 in 1946.

The Yankee slugger got off to an excellent start in his rookie season of 1939 by banging out 11 homers, 83 RBIs, batted .334, and slugged even an .500. He was a fine all-around player who fielded his position with distinction. He established four Yankee rookie fielding records in right field for putouts, total chancesgame, total chances and fewest errors. Three of these records have never been broken in over a half century.

Keller also performed well in World Series play. In the five fall classics he participated in, the strong swinging lefty rapped out 22 hits which included 5 round trippers, 18 runs scored, 18 RBIs, a batting average of .306 and a marvelous slugging average of .611 which is the eighth highest in baseball history. His best series was in his rookie year of 1939, when he connected for 3 home runs and batted .438. His slugging average of 1.188 is a record which has never been broken.

RECORD PROFILE

MICKEY CHARLES MANTLE
(The Commerce Comet, The Mick)
b. Oct. 20, 1931
NY-AL 1951-68

Number of Records Established–13

American League Records

	Years lasted before broken	Broken by:
Career Batting Records 1951-68		
Strikeouts	1,710 19	Reggie Jackson

Major League Records
Career Batting Records 1951-68
Strikeouts	1,710 11	Lou Brock

All-Star Game Records
Career Batting Records 1951-68
Strikeouts	16	**Never broken**

World Series Records

Game Batting Records

1960 RBIs	5		Same Series Bobby Richardson

7-Game Series Batting Records

1966 Runs Scored	8		Tied Tommy Leach, Pepper Martin, Billy Johnson, Bobby Richardson and was tied by Lou Brock
RBIs	10	4	Bobby Richardson

Career Batting Records 1951-68

Home Runs	18	Never broken
Runs Scored	42	Never broken
RBIs	40	Never broken
Total Bases	123	Never broken
Extra Base Hits	26	Never broken
Bases On Balls	43	Never broken
Strikeouts	54	Never broken

Summary

Mickey Mantle was the greatest switch hitter in baseball history. He led the league 27 times in various batting categories. He was a four-time home run champion, a two-time home run percentage king, and he won six runs scoring titles and four bases on balls crowns. He was a three-time slugging average leader and has won single titles in batting average and RBIs. He is one of the rare players who have won the MVP award three times, the only switch hitter to win the triple crown and his 536 home runs place him sixth on the all-time list.

Mickey was an outstanding all-around player who could play his position, center field with the best of them. He was given the task of replacing the great Joe DiMaggio and he did it with style. Four times he led the league in various fielding departments.

When the pressure was on, "The Mick," always rose to the occasion. This can easily be seen by reviewing his phenomenal achievements during his play in the world series. No one can accuse Mantle of choking under the pressure of the world series. No player in baseball history has hit more home runs, scored more runs, driven in more runs, has more total bases, extra base hit or bases on balls.

Mantle was welcomed into the Hall of Fame in 1974.

Post season Awards:

MVP 1956, 1957 and 1962
Triple Crown 1956
(52 home runs, 130 RBIs and a .353 batting average)

Career Statistics:

Years: 18
Strikeouts: 1,710
Home Run %: 6.6
At Bats: 8,102
Slugging Average: .557
RBIs:1,509
Doubles: 344
Pinch Hits: 25
Stolen Bases: 53

Home Runs: 536
Games: 2,401
Batting Average: .298
Runs Scored: 1,677
Hit: 2,415
Pinch Hit At Bats: 106
Walks: 1,734
Triples: 72

RECORD PROFILE

REGINALD MARTINEZ JACKSON

(Mr. October)
b. May 18, 1946
KC-AL, Oak-AL, Bal-AL, NY-AL, Cal-AL

Number of Records Established–41

American League Records

	Years lasted before broken	Broken by:
Career Batting Records 1967-87		
Strikeouts	2595	Never broken

Major League Records

Career Batting Records 1967-87		
Strikeouts	2595	Never broken

World Series Records

Game Batting Records		
1977 Home Runs	3	Tied Babe Ruth
Total Bases	12	Tied Babe Ruth
Runs Scored	4	Tied Babe Ruth, Earle Combs and Frank Crosetti
6-Game Series Batting Records		
1977 Doubles	6	Never broken

Home Runs	5		**Never broken**
Extra Base Hits	6		**Never broken**
Total Bases	25		**Never broken**
Runs Scored	10		**Never broken**
Slugging Average	1.250		**Never broken**

Oakland A's Club Records

Season Batting Records

1968	Home Runs	29	1	Self
	Home Run %	5.2	1	Self
	Extra Base Hits	48	1	Self
	Total Bases	250	1	Self
	Strikeouts	171	17	Jose Canseco
	Slugging Average	.462	1	Self
1969	Home Runs	47	18	Mark McGuire
	Home Run %	8.6	18	Mark McGuire
	Runs Scored	123		**Never broken**
	RBIs	118	19	Jose Canseco
	Extra Base Hits	86		**Never broken**
	Total Bases	334	19	Jose Canseco
	Slugging Average	.608	18	Mark McGuire

Career Batting Records 1967-75

Years	8	1	Bert Campaneris
At Bats	4,212	1	Bert Campaneris
Hits	1,133	1	Bert Campaneris
Singles	602	1	Bert Campaneris
Doubles	216	7	Joe Rudi
Home Runs	293		**Never broken**
Home Run %	5.9	16	Mark McGuire
Runs Scored	701	1	Bert Campaneris
RBIs	727	1	Sal Bando
Extra Base Hits	531		**Never broken**
Total Bases	2,272		**Never broken**
Bases On Balls	590	1	Sal Bando
Stolen Bases	142	1	Bert Campaneris
Strikeouts	1,123		**Never broken**
Slugging Average	.507	16	Mark McGuire

Rookie Batting Records (American League)

1968	Strikeouts 171	18	Pete Incaviglia

Summary

There are some very interesting things said about Reggie Jackson: "Reggie's a really good guy, down deep he is. . . he'd give you the shirt off his back. Of course, he'd call a press conference to announce it." (Catfish Hunter). "There's Reggie Jackson lovers and Reggie Jackson haters. I don't think he cares which way they go as long as they shout, 'Reggie.'" (Billy Hunter).

"Late in a close big game...and with the deep, baying cries from the stands rolling across the field: Reg-gie Reg-gie Reg-gie'. . . he strides to the plate and taps it with his bat and settles his batting helmet and gets his feet right and turns his glittery regard toward the pitcher, and we suddenly know that it is a different hitter we are watching now, and a different man. Get ready, everybody, it's show time." (Roger Angell).

"The advantage of playing in New York is in getting to watch Reggie Jackson play every day. And the disadvantage is in getting to watch Reggie Jackson play every day." (Graig Nettles)

"The circus is back in town," (Rick Cerone). "When everything is in place, in the proper sequence, he's awesome. In a season of four hundred and fifty at bats, maybe twelve hundred swings, you can only count on maybe twenty perfect swings a year. When he does it, I get goose pimples." (Charnley Lau).

"Reggie Jackson hit one off me that's still burrowing its way to Los Angeles." (Dan Quisenberry).

This is what Reggie Jackson has said about himself and others: "I don't want to be a hero. I don't want to be a star. It just works out that way. Anything that has to do with Reggie Jackson becomes a big thing. I represent both the underdog and the over dog in this society. It's not really an athlete's story. It is a human story. I don't want to be liked, I just want to be respected. I love competition. It motivates me, stimulates me, excites me. It is almost sexual. I just love to hit that baseball in a big game. The only reason I don't like playing in the World Series is I can't watch myself play. I was in a position where, if I failed, the fans and the press would have buried me. They gotcha, boy. They don't let you escape with minor scratches and bruises. They put scars on you here. Come to the Big Apple and have a bite. I had to either learn to digest, or choke. Babe Ruth was great. I was only lucky. Nothing can happen to me because I can hit the ball over the wall. When I can't hit the ball over the wall, they's get me too. George will get me someday."

Love him or hate him, Reggie Jackson was a great ballplayer. You really can't say he was bragging because he could and did back it up. Reggie loved the pressure, the one on one situations. . . And more times than not, he won. Players would rather have Reggie on their side than against them. He was a winner, and players felt they had a great chance at winning with Reggie swinging the bat for them.

He had the dubious distinction of striking out more times than anyone in baseball history. But this comes with the territory for all great home run hitters. When Babe Ruth retired, he too had the most strikeouts. So did Mickey Mantle and Willie Stargell. And someday soon, another future great will come along and pass Reggie on the all-time strikeout list.

Reggae did it when it counted the most – in World Series play. What a great thrill it was to see him tie Babe Ruth's three home runs in one World Series game in 1977. No other player has ever succeeded in a 6-game World Series as Reggie Jackson. He rewrote the record book in 1977, when he rapped the most doubles, home runs, extra base hits, total bases, runs scored and had the highest slugging average of any player in baseball history. These fantastic records will be in the book for a very long time. . . perhaps forever.

When Reggie left the Oakland A's in 1975, he was the greatest player that franchise ever had. Many still think he is the greatest. Mark McGuire and Jose Canseco have broken some of his records, but the great slugger still has six unbroken club records.

Jackson won the MVP award in 1973 and will soon be eligible for the Hall of Fame. That should be automatic for Mr. October who tied five and broke five of Babe Ruth's World Series records.

RECORD PROFILE

EDWARD CHARLES FORD

(Whitey Ford, Chairman of the Board)
b. Oct. 21, 1928
New York-AL 1950-67

Number of Records Established–21

American League Records

	Years lasted before broken	Broken by:
Season Pitching Title Records		
1961 Cy Young Award	1 8	Denny McLain

Major League Records
Career Pitching Title Records

1961 Cy Young Award	1 4	Sandy Koufax

All-Star Game Records
Game Pitching Records

1955 Most Hits one Inning	5	Tied Sandy Consequera

Career Pitching Records 1950-67

Losses	2	Tied Mort Cooper, Claude Passeau, Luis Tiant, and Catfish Hunter

World Series Records

4-Game Series Pitching Records

1963	Starts	2	Tied by many
	Losses	2	Tied by many

7-Game Series Pitching Records

1958	Starts	3	Jack Sanford
1960	Lowest ERA	0.000	Tied Duster Mails, Don Larsen, Clem Labine and was tied by Jack Billingham
	Shutouts	2	Tied Lew Burdette and was tied by Sandy Koufax

Career Pitching Records 1950-67

Series Played	11		Never broken
Games	22		Never broken
Games Started	22		Never broken
Wins	10		Never broken
Losses	8		Never broken
Innings	146		Never broken
Cons. Scoreless Inn.	33	20	Oral Hershiser
Bases On Balls	34		Never broken
Strikeouts	94		Never broken
Hits	13	2	Never broken

Summary

He was called, "The Chairman of the Board," and was always in control. He exuded confidence yet was never arrogant. He was as crafty a left-handed pitcher as there ever was. His lifetime winning percentage of .690 is the second highest in baseball history and he is only two percentage points away from tying Bob Caruthers for the highest winning percentage. Whitney won 236 games and lost only 106. He is easily the greatest left-handed pitcher in New York Yankee history.

One of his proudest moments came in World Series play when he spun 33 consecutive scoreless innings, breaking the record of Babe Ruth. Ford sparkled under the pressure of the fall classic. He compiled 15 World Series records and 13 have never been broken. He holds more unbroken World Series records than any pitcher in baseball.

Ford was a league leader in 15 various pitching categories and was instrumental in taking the Yankees to 11 pennants. He won the Cy Young award in 1961 when he enjoyed the best season of his career. In that year he won 25 while only losing 4 times for a super winning percentage of .862 . His next best year was in 1963, when he won 24 and lost 7. Whitey led the league in wins three times and was also a three time winning percentage leader. Twice he led the league in ERA, innings pitched, shutouts and games started.

Whitey Ford had a great attitude. He is quoted as saying, "I don't like to be made a big thing of. I just like to go someplace, and you buy one and I buy one." This humble baseball giant became a Hall of Famer in 1974.

Post season Awards

1961 Cy Young Award

Career Pitching Statistics 1950-67

Years: 16

Shutouts: 45

Games Completed: 156

Losses: 106

Relief Wins: 9

Hits: 2,766

ERA: 2.75

Saves: 10

Strikeouts: 1,956

Games Started: 438

Wins: 236

Relief Games: 60

Inning: 3,170

Win %: .690

Relief Losses: 7

Walks: 1,086

Total Games: 498

RECORD PROFILE

HENRY ALBERT BAUER

(Hank)
b. July 31, 1922
NY-AL 1948-59, KC-AL 1960-61

Number of Records Established–15

World Series Records

	Years lasted before broken	Broken by:
7-Game Series Batting Records		
1958 Most Home Runs	4	Tied Babe Ruth, Duke Snider and was tied by Gene Tenace
6-Game Series Fielding Records-RF		
1953 Most Putouts	14	Tied Max Flack, was tied by Lou Piniella
7-Game Series Fielding Records-RF		
1956 Most Errors	1 8	Mickey Mantle

Career Batting Records 1948-61			
Cons. Games Hit			
Safely	17		**Never broken**
Games Played	53	5	Yogi Berra
Career Fielding Records-RF 1948-61			
Putouts	76		**Never broken**
Total Chances	78		**Never broken**
Total Chances w/o Errors	51		**Never broken**

New York Yankee Club Records

Rookie Fielding Records-RF				
1949	Double Plays	3	18	Steve Whitaker
Season Fielding Records-RF				
1951	Fewest Errors	2	13	Roger Maris
1953	Fewest Errors	2	11	Roger Maris
	Fielding Average	.992	11	Roger Maris
1954	Fewest Errors	2	10	Roger Maris
Career Fielding Records-RF 1948-59				
	Fewest Errors			
	Per Years	3.5	7	Roger Maris
	Fielding Ave.	.983	7	Roger Maris

Summary

Hank Bauer replaced Tommy Henrich in right field and became part of a new and exciting Yankee outfield which included Mickey Mantle and Gene Wooding. This may not sound as exciting as the previous outfield trio of Joe DiMaggio, Charlie Keller and Tommy Henrich...or the trio of outfielders who preceeded them (Babe Ruth, Earle Combs and Bob Meusel). All three groups of Yankee outfielders won many pennants and World Series for the Yankees and it would be interesting to see which group would get the most votes for the greatest Yankee outfield.

Bauer did more than his share to help the Yankees continue their winning tradition. During the twelve years he proudly put on the Yankee uniform, Bauer was instrumental in helping the team win 9 pennants and 7 World Series.

Bauer was an ex-marine and as tough and gritty as they came. Someone once described him as having a face which looked like a clenched fist. He wore that marine crew cut and had the hustle of a Pete Rose. He was a complete player who could hit, run and throw with equal ability. He wa a clutch performer who never wilted under pressure. This can easily be seen by his outstanding World Series performance.

In his 9 World Series events, Bauer participated in 53 games (4th), 188 at bats (6th), 46 hits (5th), 3 triples (4th), 7 homers (10th), 21 runs (10th) and 24 RBIs, (7th). His most outstanding World Series record is his 17 game hitting streak that no other player in baseball history has ever come close to breaking. He is also proud of tieing Babe Ruth and Duke Snider for most home runs in a 7-game series.

The ex-marine was an excellent right fielder and to this day has recorded more putouts, total chances and total chances without making an error than any player in baseball history. As a Yankkee right fielder, only Roger Maris has shown a two point higher fielding average and has made fewer errors than Bayer, (3.3 to 3.5 per year).

Career Statistics

Years: 14

Strikeouts: 638

Home Run %: 3.2

At Bats: 5,145

Slugging Average: .439

RBIs: 703

Doubles: 229

Pinch Hits: 36

Stolen Bases: 50

Home Runs: 164

Games: 1,544

Batting Average: .277

Runs Scored: 833

Hits: 1,424

Pinch Hit At Bats: 121

Walks: 519

Triples: 57

RECORD PROFILE

ROBERTO WALKER CLEMENTE
Pit-NL 1955-72
b. Aug. 18, 1934, d. Dec. 31, 1972

Number of Records Established–15

National League Records

Fielding Records-RF 1955-72	Years lasted before broken	Broken by:
Games Played	2,370	Never broken

Major League Records

Career Fielding Records-RF 1955-72

Games Played	2,370	2	Al Kaline

All-Star Game Records

Game Batting Records

1967 Strikeouts	4	Never broken

Pittsburgh Pirates Club Records

Season Fielding Records-RF

1971 Fewest Errors	2	13	Lee Lacy

Career Batting Records 1955-72

Most Years	18	10	Willie Stargell
Games	2,433		Never broken
At Bats	9,454		Never broken
Hits	3,000		Never broken
Singles	2,154		Never broken
Strikeouts	1,230	10	Willie Stargell

Career Fielding Records-RF 1955-72

Years	18	Never broken
Putouts	4,696	Never broken
Assists	266	Never broken
Errors	140	Never broken
Total Chances	5,102	Never broken

Summary

Roberto Clemente will go down in baseball history as one of its greatest all-around right fielders. No other National League player has played in as many games as Clemente and only Al Kaline in the American League has played more games in right field.

In a fabulous 18-year career, Clemente batted over .300 thirteen times, twice he batted over .350, and four times he had more than 200 hits in one season. In all, he led the league in various batting categories seven times and was a four-time batting average champion.

Defensively, he was one of the very best. He possessed one of the strongest and most accurate arms of any outfielder in baseball. Nine times he led the league in various fielding departments.

In two World Series appearances, Roberto had a composite batting average of .362 which ranks sixth best on the all-time list. He came to bat a total of 58 times and smacked 21 hits of which two were homers, two doubles, and one triple. He scored 4 runs, drove in 7, and had a slugging average of .534.

Clement won the MVP award in 1966 and was inducted into the Hall of Fame in 1973, a year after his death caused by an airplane crash.

Pirate fans will always remember him as one of their greatest players. No other Pirate has played as many games, had more at bats, or base hits as Roberto. And no other Pirate right fielder has played as many years, games or had as many putouts, assists, and total chances.

Post season Awards

1966 MVP

Career Statistics

Years: 18   Home Runs: 240
Strikeouts: 1,230   Games: 2,433
Home Run %: 2.5   Batting Average: .317
At Bats: 9,454   Runs Scored: 1,416
Slugging Average: .475   Hits: 3,000
RBIs: 1,305   Pinch Hit At Bats: 73
Doubles: 440   Walks: 621
Pinch Hits: 19   Triples: 166
Stolen Bases: 83

Quote About Roberto Clemente
by Roger Angell

"Roberto Clemente led the Pirates to the 1971 World Championship and demonstrated a kind of baseball that none of us had ever seen before-throwing, running and hitting at something close to the level of absolute perfection."

RECORD PROFILE

JOSEPH MICHAEL MEDWICK

(Ducky, Muscles)
b. Nov. 24, 1911, d. Mar. 21, 1975
StL-NL 1932-40, Bkn-NL 1940-43, NY-NL 1943-45,
Bos-NL 1945, Bkn-NL 1946, StL-NL 1947-48

Number of Records Established–32

National League Records

Season Batting Records	Years lasted before broken	Broken by:
1936 Most Doubles	64	Never broken

All-Star Game Records

Game Batting Records			
1934 Home Runs	1	7	Arky Vaughn
RBIs	3	3	Lou Gehrig
1937 Hits	4		Tied by Ted Williams and Carl Yastremski
Doubles	2		Tied Al Simmons and was tied by Ted Kluszewski and Ernie Banks

Total Bases	6	4	Arky Vaughn
Extra Base Hits	2		Tied by many

Career Batting Records 1932-48

Most RBIs	5	6	Joe DiMaggio
Triples	1	29	Willie Mays
Extra Base Hits	3	16	Ted Williams

World Series Records

Game Batting Records

1934 Most Hits	4	48	Paul Molitar

St. Louis Cardinals Club Records

Rookie Batting Records

1933 At Bats	595	10	Lou Klein
Doubles	40		**Never broken**
Home Runs	18	3	Johnny Mize
Extra Base Hits	68		**Never broken**
RBIs	98	20	Ray Jablonski
Strikeouts	56	4	Don Gutteridge
Total Bases	296		**Never broken**

Rookie Fielding Records-LF

1933 Fewest Errors	7	9	Stan Musial
Fielding Average	.980	9	Stan Musial

Season Batting Records

1934 Strikeouts	83	19	Steve Bilko
1935 Games	154	27	Ken Boyer
1936 Games	154	26	Ken Boyer
Doubles	64		**Never broken**
1937 Games	154	25	Ken Boyer
RBIs	154		**Never broken**

Season Fielding Records-LF

1936 Fielding Average	.986	1	Self
1937 Fielding Average	.988	24	Charlie James

Career Batting Records 1932-40, 47-48

Doubles	375	15	Stan Musial

Career Fielding Records-LF 1932-40, 47-48

Putouts	2,412	31	Lou Brock

| Total Chances | 2,557 | 31 | Lou Brock |
| Fielding Average | .984 | 15 | Stan Musial |

Summary

"Ducky" Joe Medwick, the man who hit more doubles in a season than any other National League player, completed a marvelous 17-year career with a .324 batting average.

He enters this record book because he is one of the few players who has successfully broken a Babe Ruth record. His shining moment came in the 1934 All-Star game when he batted in 3 runs. In 1937, he again took away a record from the Babe when he had 6 total bases in one game.

Some called him "Muscles" while others called him "Ducky." Pitchers called him awesome as he led the league in various batting categories 13 times. Twice he led the league in hits, three times in doubles, three in RBIs, and he had single titles in at bats, triples, home runs, runs scored, batting average and slugging average. Most amazing is that he batted over .300 eleven times in succession and 14 times in 17 years. His highest batting averages were: .374, .353 and .351.

Medwick enjoyed his finest hour in 1937, when he won both the triple crown and MVP award. In that year he batted .374, ripped 237 hits, 56 doubles, 31 homers, drove in 154 runs and slugged a solid .641. He became a Hall of Famer in 1968.

He began his career with the St. Louis Cardinals in 1933, and what a start it was. He established seven Cardinal rookie records which included the most at bats, doubles, home runs, extra base hits, RBIs, strikeouts and total bases. To this day, no other Cardinal rookie has broken his records for doubles, extra base hits or total bases. Medwick also established two rookie fielding records as a left fielder which lasted 9 years before they were broken by Stan Musial. When Medwick had completed his rookie sea-

son, he had made the fewest errors and had the highest
fielding average of any previous Cardinal rookie left fielder.

Medwick is most proud of his National League doubles record which he set in 1936 and has never been broken.
Also high on his list of achievements are the 154 RBIs he
mustered in 1937, that no other Cardinal player has ever
broken. He became a Hall of Famer in 1968.

Post season Awards

1937 MVP and Triple Crown

Career Statistics

Years: 17

Strikeouts: 551

Home Run %: 2.7

At Bats: 7,635

Slugging Average: .505

RBIs: 1,383

Doubles: 540

Pinch Hits: 22

Stolen Bases: 42

Home Runs: 205

Games: 1,984

Batting Average: .324

Runs Scored: 1,198

Hits: 2,471

Pinch Hit At Bats: 107

Walks: 437

Triples: 113

Quote From Joe Medwick

"I know why they threw that stuff at me. What I can't
figure out is why they brought it to the ball park in the first
place." (After Tiger fans pelted him with fruit, bottles, and
trash during the 1934 World Series).

RECORD PROFILE

JACKIE ROBINSON
b. Jan. 31, 1919, d. Oct. 24, 1972
Bkn-NL 1947-56

Number of Records Established–15

National League Records

	Years lasted before broken		Broken by:
Rookie Fielding Records-1B			
1947 Double Plays	144		**Never broken**
Season Fielding Records-2B			
1950 Double Plays	133	1	Self
1951 Double Plays	137	10	Bill Mazeroski
Fielding Average	.991	22	Tito Fuentes

World Series Records
Game Batting Records

1952 Bases On Balls	4	Tied Fred Clarke, Robert Hoblitzell, Ross Youngs, Babe Ruth and was tied by Doug DeCinces

Brooklyn Dodgers Club Records

Rookie Batting Records

1947	Bases On Balls	74	6	Junior Gilliam

Rookie Fielding Records-1B

1947	Double Prays	144		Never broken
	Fielding Average	.989		Tied by Jake Daubert

Season Batting Records

1951	Games	154	11	Maury Wills

Season Fielding Records-2B

1950	Double Plays	133	1	Self
	Fielding Average	.986	1	Self
1951	Double Plays	137		Never broken
	Fielding Average	.992		Never broken

Career Fielding Records-2B 1947-56

	Double Plays	582	28	Davey Lopez
	Fielding Average	.983		Never broken

Summary

Jackie Robinson will always be remembered as the man who broke the color barrier in baseball. It took an exceptional human being to do what Robinson did in 1947. He survived the taunts and threats of many people, players, and fans alike. He controlled his temper when players called him "nigger" and while he was often tempted to fight back, he always managed to keep his composure and rise above the abuse. It was an extremely long and frustrating season in 1947, yet Jackie kept his cool and played excellent baseball, good enough to earn him Rookie of The Year honors.

He was an exciting player to watch. He was everywhere, attacking with the bat, on the base paths and with his glove. He truly excelled in all three areas. His .311 career batting average proved that he could hit and there was no doubts about his fielding. In addition, he was one of baseball's greatest base runners.

As a second baseman, Robinson led the league in various fielding departments 10 times and his rookie double play record as a first baseman has never been broken.

Jackie had excellent bat control and was one of the most difficult players to strike out. During his career, he came to bat 4,877 times and only struck out 291 times. He won the batting average crown in only his third year of play. In that year he batted a solid .342.

Robinson proudly put on the Dodger blue for ten years and during that time led the team to six pennants. He was a leader, a winner and as tough a player as they come. A tremendous producer in the clutch, he excelled under pressure situations, especially in the World Series where he is in the top ten in doubles, runs scored and bases on balls. He played in 38 World Series games, had 137 at bats with 32 hits.

Jackie opened the way for other black players to play major league ball. There is no telling how much of a setback Black players would have suffered if Robinson had not succeeded. He was a true inspiration to his race and to the game. To this day, he remains the Dodgers greatest second baseman. He was inducted into the Hall of Fame in 1962.

Post season Awards

1947 Rookie of The Year
1949 MVP

Career Statistics

Years: 10

Strikeouts: 291

Home Run %: 2.8

At Bats: 4,877

Slugging Average: .474

RBIs: 734

Doubles: 273

Pinch Hits: 7

Stolen Bases: 197

Home Runs: 137

Games: 1,382

Batting Average: .311

Runs Scored: 947

Hits: 1,518

Pinch Hit At Bats: 40

Walks: 740

Triples: 54

Quotes From Jackie Robinson

"I'm not concerned with your liking or disliking me. . . . Aall I ask is that you respect me as a human being."

Quotes About Jackie Robinson

"All of us, we had to wait for Jackie." (Joe Black, teammate)

"Jackie Robinson is the loneliest man I have ever seen in sports." (Jimmy Cannon)

"Like a few, very few athletes. . . Robinson did not merely play at center stage. He was center stage; and wherever he walked center stage moved with him." (Roger Kahn)

"This is the United States of America and one citizen has as much right to play as another." (Ford Frick, Commissioner)

"Thinking about the things that happened, I don't know any other ball player who could have done what he did. To be able to hit with everybody yelling at him. He had to block all that out, block out everything but his ball that is coming in at a hundred miles an hour. To do what he did has got to be the most tremendous thing I've ever seen in sports." (PeeWee Reese)

"Give me five players like Robinson and a pitcher, and I'll beat any nine-man team in baseball." (Charlie Dressen, Dodger Manager)

"Robinson could hit and bunt and steal and run. He had intimidating skills, and he burned with a dark fire. He wanted passionately to win. He bore the burden of a pioneer and the weight made him more strong. If one can be certain of anything in baseball, it is that we shall not look upon his like again." (Roger Kahn)

"If there is an unfilled obligation in the case of baseball vs. Jackie Robinson, the debt belongs to baseball, which can never pay off in full." (Harold Weissman, sportswriter)

"Every time I look at my pocketbook, I see Jackie Robinson." (Willie Mays)

Jackie Robinson to Branch Rickey: "Are you looking for a Negro who is afraid to fight back?"

Branch Rickey: "No. I'm looking for a ballplayer with the guts enough not to fight back."

RECORD PROFILE

WALTER ARTHUR EVERS
(Hoot)
b. Feb. 8, 1921
Det–AL 1941-52, Bos–AL 1952-54, NY–NL 1954, Det–AL
1954, Bal–AL 1955, Cle-AL 1955-56, Bal-AL 1956

Number of Records Established– 8

Season Fielding Records-LF		Years lasted before broken	Broken by:
1949 Fielding Average	.994	1	Self
1950 Fielding Average	.997	21	Roy White

Detroit Tigers Club Records

Season Fielding Records-LF

1947	Total Chances/game	3.0	29	Ron LeFlore
1948	Total Chances/game	3.0	28	Ron LeFlore
1949	Fewest Errors	2	1	Self
	Fielding Average	.994	1	Self
1950	Fewest Errors	1		Tied by Jim Delsing, Charlie Maxwell and Steve Kemp
	Fielding Average	.997		Tied by Charlie Maxwell

Summary

In 1919, Babe Ruth played his first full season as an outfielder. He played left field and did an unbelievable job by leading the league in fielding average while committing only two errors. His record for fewest errors by a left fielder would last 31 years before being broken. Can you name the American League left fielder who broke this record? Walter (Hoot) Evers can proudly tell his grandchildren that it was he who performed this mighty task. In 1950, Evers became the first American League left fielder to play a full season while making only one error. This mark would last 21 years before Roy White of the Yankees became the first left fielder not to make an error.

Evers played major league ball for twelve years, mostly with the Detroit Tigers. He was a strong defensive left fielder and a consistent hitter. In his first full season in 1947, he batted a respectable .296 and became a .300 hitter the following year when he banged out 169 hits and came in with a solid .314 batting average. He again hit over .300 in 1949, coming in at a .303 clip. He enjoyed his best season in 1950 when he connected for 170 hits, eleven of them were triples, which led the league. His slugging average that year was a solid .551 as a result of his career high 21 home runs and 35 doubles to go along with his league leading eleven triples. His batting average was a super .323.

Hoot Evers placed eight records in the book; three of them he broke himself. Only two players, Roy White and Ron LeFlore, were able to break his records. Jim Delsing, Charlie Maxwell and Steve Kemp succeeded in only tieing Evers' record.

Career Statistics

Years: 12
Strikeouts: 420
Home Run %: 2.6
At Bats: 3,801
Slugging Average: .426
RBIs: 565
Doubles: 187
Pinch Hits: 16
Stolen Bases: 45

Home Runs: 98
Games: 1,142
Batting Average: .278
Runs Scored: 556
Hits: 1,055
Pinch Hit At Bats: 76
Walks: 415
Triples: 41

RECORD PROFILE

BILLY MARTIN

(Billy)

b. May 16, 1928, d. Dec. 25, 1990

NY-AL 1950-57, KC-AL 1957, Det-AL 1958, Cle-AL 1959,
Cin-NL 1960, Mil-NL 1961, Min-AL 1961

Number of Records Established–9

World Series Records

		Years lasted before broken	Broken by:
6-Game Series Batting Records			
1953	Most Hits	12	Never broken
	Triples	2	Tied George Rohe and Bob Meusel
	Extra Base Hits	5	Tied Babe Ruth and Chick Hafey
	Total Bases	23 24	Reggie Jackson
	RBIs	8 6	Ted Kluszewski
	Batting Average	.500	Tied Dave Robertson

New York Yankee Club Records

Rookie Fielding Records-2B

1952 Fewest Errors	9		Never broken
Fielding Average	.984		Never broken

Season Fielding Records-2B

1953 Fewest Errors		12 14	Horace Clark

Summary

Billy Martin was the type of scrappy player all managers like to have on their teams. He was the "get down and dirty" type player who was always hustling and playing hard.

He didn't have the grace of a Bobby Richardson or Willie Randolph or other great Yankee second basemen, but he had the courage to stay in front of hard hit balls and was not shy about turning the double play.

He was always in the thick of the action and had his share of disputes and tussles with opposing players. Getting into fights on and off the field would be a problem that would follow him wherever he went. But he loved baseball and when his playing days were over, he became an outstanding manager. He had that gift of being able to motivate his players and get the most out of them. He often took second division teams and turned them into first division finishers and pennant winners.

Billy Martin was always a take-charge guy. He was an outstanding player under pressure and an exceptionally good clutch hitter. His greatest moments came during the 1953 World Series when he rewrote the record book for a 6-game series. He established six records which included most hits-12, triples-2, extra base hits-5, total bases-23, RBIs-8 and batting average-.500. Certainly not bad for a .257 lifetime hitter.

Martin's 12 hits for a 6-game series is a record that is still unbroken. His two triples tied him with George Rohe and Bob Meusel and his 5 extra base hits tied him with Babe Ruth and Chick Hafey. When he batted .500, he became the second player in baseball history to accomplish this feat. Only Dave Robertson had done this before or after him.

Martin's 8 RBIs would last 6 years before Ted Kluzewski would best his performance and Martin's 23 total bases would not be bettered until Reggie Jackson would shatter it 24 years later.

The record Billy Martin is most proud of is his 23 total base mark because he took that one away from Babe Ruth. What a wonderful thrill it was for him to be able to say that he broke a Babe Ruth record.

He did well as a rookie in 1952 and surprised the Yankees by breaking rookie fielding marks at second base. His 9 errors were the lowest number ever made by a Yankee rookie second baseman and his .984 fielding average was the highest ever. These marks still stand today.

Career Statistics

Years: 11
Strikeouts: 355
Home Run %: 1.9
At Bats: 3,419
Slugging Average: .367
RBIs: 333
Doubles: 137
Pinch Hits: 3
Stolen Bases: 34

Home Runs: 64
Games: 1,021
Batting Average: .257
Runs Scored: 425
Hits: 877
Pinch Hit At Bats: 44
Walks: 187
Triples: 28

Quotes From Billy Martin:

"If you stand next to Gaylord Perry, he smells like a drug store."

"The rules are made by me, but I don't have to follow them."

"I believe if God ever managed, He would have been very aggressive, the way I manage."

"There's no excuse for happy losers."

RECORD PROFILE

WESLEY FERRELL
(Cheek)

b. Feb. 2, 1908, d. Dec. 9, 1976
Cle-AL 1927-33, Bos-AL 1934-37, Was-AL 1937-38,
NY-AL 1938-39, Bkn-NL 1940, Bos-NL 1941

Number of Records Established–4

American League Records

Season Batting Records	Years lasted before broken	Broken by:
1931 Most Home Runs By Pitcher	9	Never broken
Career Batting Records 1927-41		
Home Runs By Pitcher	38	Never broken

Major League Records
Season Batting Records

1931 Home Runs By Pitcher	9	Never broken
Career Batting Records 1927-41		
Home Runs By Pitcher	38	Never broken

166 Summary Wes Ferrell

Summary

Wes Ferrell was one of baseball's greatest hitting pitchers. He first became famous for breaking Babe Ruth's record for most home runs in a season hit by a pitcher. In 1915 the Babe had hit 4 round trippers and this remained a record until Farrell would belt 9 home runs in 1931. Farrell collected 38 home runs in his career to also capture the career home run record for pitchers. Both marks are also major league records and have never been broken.

Farrell was also a tremendous pitcher, one who has sorely been overlooked by the Hall of Fame voters. Six times he had 20 or more wins in one season yet, surprisingly, there are many pitchers in the Hall of Fame who cannot claim this achievement.

In Ferrell's first four full seasons, he won 20 or more games four times in a row. He was 21-10 in 1929, 25-13 in 1930, 22-12 in 1931, and 23-13 in 1932. He dropped off to 11-12 in 1933 and came with a smart 14-5 mark in 1934, and then was 25-14 in 1935, and 20-15 in 1936. His career was coming to a close after that and in the final 5 years while pitching part time, he compiled a record of 32-32. In all, the 6'2" 200 pound righthander won 193 and lost 128 for a fine winning percentage of .601. Again there are many pitchers in the Hall of Fame with less than a .600 winning percentage. Perhaps even more important is the number of wins above the .500 mark. In that area, Ferrell has posted 65 more wins than losses which place him 30th on the all-time list. There are 17 pitchers in the Hall of Fame who rank below Ferrell in this most important category. They are: Addie Joss, Catfish Hunter, Burleigh Grimes, Dazzy Vance, Early Wynn, Waite Hoyt, Jesse Haines, Pud Galvin, Rube Waddell, Don Drysdale, Red Faber, Robin Roberts, Al Spalding, Ted Lyons, Rube Marquard, Hoyt Wilhelm and Eppa Rixey.

Only 16 pitchers in the Hall of Fame have won more than 20 or more games in one season more times than Ferrell. Some of the more notable pitchers who could not match Ferrell in this area are: Catfish Hunter, Bob Gibson, Rube Wadell, Red Ruffing, Lefty Gomez, Dizzy Dean, Sandy Koufax, Whitey Ford and 17 others.

Another category which shows a pitcher's greatness is the number of times they were league leaders in various pitching categories. In this stat, Ferrell was a league leader 14 times. This ranks him ahead of 22 of the pitchers in the Hall of Fame.

Getting back to his hitting prowess, Ferrell had a lifetime batting average of .279 which places him very high amongst all pitchers. In 1,176 at bats, he accumulated 329 hits. Only Red Ruffing and Warren Spahn have had more hits.

Career Statistics

Years: 15
Losses: 128
ERA: 4.04
Games Started: 323
Innings: 2623
Walks: 1040
Shutouts: 17
Relief Losses: 9

Wins: 193
Winning Percentage: .601
Games: 374
Games Completed: 227
Hits: 2845
Strikeouts: 985
Relief Wins: 11
Saves: 13

RECORD PROFILE

DELBERT BERNARD UNSER

b. Dec. 9, 1944
Was-AL 1968-71, Cle-AL 1972, Phi-NL 1973-74, NY-NL
1975-76, Mon-NL 1976-78, Phi-NL 1979-82

Number of Records Established–5

American League Records

	Years lasted before broken	Broken by:
Season Fielding Records-RF		
1971 Most Putouts	394	Never broken

Major League Records

Season Fielding Records-RF

1971 Most Putouts	394	Never broken

Washington Senators Club Records

Season Fielding Records-RF

1971 Most Putouts	394	Never broken

New York Mets Club Records

Season Fielding Records-CF

1976 Fewest Errors	1	Never broken
Fielding Average	.995	Never broken

Summary

Not many players can say that every record they have
ever created in major league baseball, has never been broken. But little known baseball dynamo Del Unser can say
this. He toiled in the big leagues for 15 years going back
and forth with four different teams. He was known for his
outstanding defensive talents but only carried a .250 bat.
Yet he can be very proud to tell anyone willing to listen,
that he broke a record held by Babe Ruth. Yes, it was in the
fielding departments as all of his records are.

In 1923, Babe Ruth set a fielding record for right fielders when he registered 378 putouts. Al Kaline would tie
Ruth's record in 1961, but it would take Del Unser to break
it with 394 putouts in 1971. Not only was this a new
American League record but also a major league mark.
Ruth did not hold the major league record but it was held
by another Babe, Babe Herman. Herman had recorded 392
putouts in 1932, and now Unser had his record as well. So a
fabulous trivia question would be: What little known outfielder broke the records of two players who were called
Babe? And who were these two Babes? Unser can also be
proud of the fact that none of his fielding records have ever
been broken.

Del Unser was a traveling man. He began his career
in 1968 with the old Washington Senators and stayed with
them until 1971. His high mark with them was in 1969
when he led the league in triples with 8 and batted .286. He
was with Cleveland in 1972 and then put in two years with
the Phillies in 1973 and 1974. He enjoyed National League
pitching better than American League as he clubbed 11
home runs each year and raised his batting average to .289
in 1973.

Unser was shipped off to the New York Mets in 1975
and had a good year with them as he batted .294 with 10
home runs. He split the 1976 season with the Mets and

Expos and had his highest home run production when he knocked an even dozen over the fences. He stayed with the Expos through 1977 and 1978, clubbed another dozen home runs in 1977, and batted a respectable .273. He ended his career with the Phillies from 1979 through 1982.

Unser helped the Phillies win the pennant and World Series in 1980. During the league championship series (playoffs), he contributed 2 hits and 5 at bats, and in the World Series he came to bat 6 times and had 3 hits for a neat .500 batting average. Two of his World Series hits were doubles.

The 1980 World Series were very exciting for Del Unser. It was the first and only series he had ever played. After the Phillies had won the first game from the Kansas City Royals 7-6, they were trailing by 4 runs in the eighth inning when doubles by pinch hitter Unser and Mike Schmidt won the game. In game 5, the Phillies were again behind when Unser again doubled as a pinch hitter, tying the score in the 9th and he scored the winning run on a single by Manny Trill. The Phillies won the series 4 games to 2. This would be the most satisfying time in Del Unser's career.

Career Statistics

Years: 15

Strikeouts: 675

Home Run %: 1.7

At Bats: 5,215

Slugging Average: .358

RBIs: 481

Doubles: 179

Pinch Hits: 54

Stolen Bases: 64

Home Runs: 87

Games: 1,799

Batting Average: .258

Runs Scored: 617

Hits: 1,344

Pinch Hit At Bats: 264

Walks: 481

Triples: 42

RECORD PROFILE

CHARLES LEO HARTNETT

(Gabby)
b. Dec.20, 1900, d. Dec. 20, 1972
Chi-NL 1922-40, NY-NL 1941

Number of Records Established-33

National League Records

	Years lasted before broken	Broken by:
Career Fielding Records-Catcher 1922-41		
Games Played	1,790	6	Al Lopez
Putouts	7,292	29	John Roseboro
Double Plays	173		**Never broken**
Total Chances	8,685	33	Johnny Edwards

Major League Records

Career Fielding Records-Catcher 1922-41

Games Played	1,790	6	Al Lopez
Putouts	7,292	5	Bill Dickey

All-Star Game Records

Game Batting Records

1933 Games Played	1	1	Self & many

1934	Games Played	2	1	Self & many
1935	Games Played	3	1	Self & many
1936	Games Played	4	1	Self & many
	Triples	1	42	Rod Carew
1937	Games Played	5	1	Lou Gehrig, Charlie Gehringer and Joe Cronin

Career Batting Records 1922-41

Games Played	5	1	Same as above
Triples	1	36	Rod Carew

World Series Records

4-Game Series Fielding Records-Catcher

1932	Most Assists	5	Never broken

Chicago Cubs Club Records

Season Fielding Records-Catcher

1928	Fewest Errors	6	6	Self
	Fielding Average	.989	6	Self
1930	Putouts	646	27	Cal Neeman
	Fielding Average	.989	4	Self
1933	Fielding Average	.989	1	Self
1934	Fewest Errors	3	3	Self
	Fielding Average	.996		Never broken
1937	Fewest Errors	2		Never broken
	Fielding Average	.996		Never broken

Career Fielding Records-Catcher 1922-40

Putouts	6,857		Never broken
Assists	1,177		Never broken
Double Plays	168		Never broken
Total Chances	8,161		Never broken
Fielding Average	.983	33	Randy Hundley
Most Years	15		Never broken

Career Batting Records 1922-40

Most Home Runs	231	31	Ernie Banks
Pinch Hit At Bats	118	7	Dom Dellasandra
Pinch Hits	29	7	Dom Dellasandra

Summary

Gabby Hartnett was an outstanding catcher with a lifetime batting average of .297. His most productive season was in 1937, when he belted enemy pitchers for a solid .354 batting average. In 1935 he did almost as well with a blazing .344 batting average. So good was Hartnett, that he was voted to the All-Star team five years in a row, a record which put him past Babe Ruth in the number of All-Star games played.

Gabby was a super defensive catcher and led the National League catchers in fielding a record 30 times. From 1934 to 1937 he led the league in fielding average. He made only two errors in 1937 for a fantastic .996 fielding average. When he retired in 1941, he had put in more games behind the plate, made more putouts, double plays and total chances than any catcher in National League history.

In the 1932 World Series, the sure-handed catcher made five assists to set another record which still stands today.

Hartnett played all but one year of his career with the Chicago Cubs and remains as the Cubs' greatest catcher. No Cubs catcher has played as many years, had more putouts, assists, double plays, and total chances than Gabby. His fielding average record stood 33 years before it was broken by Randy Hudley.

Gabby was also a fine long ball hitter and when he retired he had hit more home runs than any previous Chicago player. This mark stood 31 years before Ernie Banks would hit more.

Gabby Hartnett won the MVP award in 1935 and was voted into the Hall of Fame in 1955.

Career Statistics

Years: 20
Strikeouts: 697
Home Run %: 3.7
At Bats: 6,432
Slugging Average: .489
RBIs: 1,179
Doubles: 396
Pinch Hits: 39
Stolen Bases: 28

Home Runs: 236
Games: 1,990
Batting Average: .297
Runs Scored: 867
Hits: 1,912
Pinch Hit At Bats: 144
Walks: 703
Triples: 64

RECORD PROFILE

FRANK FRANCIS FRISCH

(Frankie, The Fordham Flash)
b. Sept. 9, 1898, d. Mar. 12, 1973
NY-NL 1919-26, StL-NL 1927-37

Number of Records Established–47

National League Records

	Years lasted before broken	Broken by:
Season Fielding Records-2B		
1927 Assists	641	**Never broken**
Total Chances	1,059	**Never broken**
Career Fielding Records-2B 1919-37		
Games Played	1,775 10	Billy Herman
Putouts	4,348 10	Billy Herman
Assists	6,026 35	Bill Mazeroski
Total Chances	10,654 10	Billy Herman
Double Plays	1,060 10	Billy Herman
Fielding Average	.972 26	Red Schoendienst

Major League Fielding Records-2B

Season Fielding Records

1927 Assists	641	**Never broken**

Total Chances	1,059		Never broken

Career Fielding Records 1919-37

Fielding Average	.972	6	Charlie Gehringer

All-Star Game Records

Game Batting Records

1933	Hits	2	1	Al Simmons
	Games Played	1	1	Self & many
	Home Runs	1	8	Arky Vaughn
	Extra Base Hits	1	1	Al Simmons
	Total Bases	5	4	Lou Gehrig
	Runs Scored	2	1	Self & Al Simmons
1934	Games Played	2	1	By many
	Runs Scored	3	12	Ted Williams

Career Batting Records 1919-37

Games Played	2	1	By many
At Bats	8	1	Al Simmons
Hits	4	1	Al Simmons
Runs Scored	4	8	Arky Vaughn
RBIs	2	4	Lou Gehrig
Singles	2	1	Bill Terry
Home Runs	2	26	Ted Williams
Total Bases	10	4	Charlie Gehringer
Extra Base Hits	2	1	Al Simmons

Career Fielding Records-2B 1919-37

Putouts	5	1	Charlie Gehringer
Assists	4	4	Charlie Gehringer

World Series Records

Game Batting Records

1921	Hits	4	61	Paul Molitar
	Runs	3	5	Babe Ruth

Game Fielding Records-3B

1921	Assists	6 2	Dave Bancroft

5-Game Series Fielding Records-2B

1922	Assists	20 21	Joe Gordon

6-Game Series Fielding Records-2B

1923	Putouts	17 36	Charlie Neal

7-Game Series Batting Records

1924	Doubles	4 10	Pete Fox
	Extra Base Hits	5 10	Pete Fox

8-Game Series Base Running Records

1921	Stolen Bases	3	Tied Ty Cobb

Career Batting Records 1919-37

	Games Played	50 17	Joe DiMaggio
	At Bats	197 17	Joe DiMaggio
	Hits	58 29	Yogi Berra
	Singles	45 29	Yogi Berra
	Doubles	10	Tied by Yogi Berra

Career Fielding Records-2B 1919-37

	Putouts	105	**Never broken**
	Assists	137	**Never broken**
	Total Chances	249	**Never broken**

Summary

Of Frisch's 47 records, 34 were established in All-Star and World Series play. No player has surpassed his career total of putouts, assists, and total chances at second base during World Series competition. He was a superior defensive second baseman who led the National League nine times in various fielding categories. Also unbroken are his major league records for one season in assists and total chances.

But "The Fordham Flash," could do a lot more than just flash the leather. He was an outstanding stick man who turned in a career batting average of .316. He hit over .300 thirteen times, doing it eleven times in a row from 1921 to 1931.

Among his other talents, he could steal bases with the best of them. He won three stolen base titles and swiped 419 in all.

Frisch led the league in hits in 1923 with 223 while batting a smart .348. He led the league in runs scored in 1924 and batted .328. He collected 208 hits in 1927 with a .337 average and led the league in stolen bases with 48. He also had 211 hits in 1921 and led the league in stolen bases in 1921 with 49.

He began his career with the New York Giants and participated in 4 consecutive World Series from 1921 to 1924. He was moved to the Cardinals in 1927 and helped them win 4 pennants as well. In his 8 World Series, he ranks 8th in games played, 4th in at bats, 3rd in hits, tied for first in doubles, 4th in triples and 6th in steals. He compiled a .294 batting average.

Frisch was voted an MVP in 1931 and was inducted into the Hall of Fame in 1947.

Career Statistics

Years: 19
Strikeouts: 272
Home Run %: 1.2
At Bats: 9,112
Slugging Average: .432
RBIs: 1,244
Doubles: 466
Pinch Hits: 12
Stolen Bases: 419

Home Runs: 105
Games: 2,311
Batting Average: .316
Runs Scored: 1,532
Hits: 2,880
Pinch Hit At Bats: 47
Walks: 728
Triples: 138

Quotes From Frankie Frisch

"You don't like or dislike your players. . . there's no room for sentiment in baseball if you want to win." (Spoken as a manager)

"There's nothing tough about playing third. All a guy needs is a strong arm and a strong chest."

RECORD PROFILE

LAWRENCE PETER BERRA

(Yogi)
b. May 12, 1925
NY-AL 1946-65

Number of Records Established–32

American League Records

	Years lasted before broken	Broken by:
Season Batting Title Records		
1955 Most MVP titles	3	Tied Jimmie Fox, Joe DiMaggio, and was tied by Mickey Mantle
Season Fielding Records-Catcher		
1958 Fewest Errors	0	Tied Buddy Rosar, Pete Daley, & Lou Berberet
Fielding Average	1.000	Same as above
Career Fielding Records-Catcher 1946-65		

| Putouts | 8,711 | 11 | Bill Freehan |
| Total Chances | 9,619 | 11 | Bill Freehan |

Major League Records

Season Batting Title Records

| 1955 Most MVP titles | 3 | Tied Jimmie Foxx, Joe DiMaggio, Stan Musial, Roy Campanella and was tied by Mickey Mantle |

Season Fielding Records-Catcher

| 1958 Fewest Errors | 0 | Tied Buddy Rosar, Pete Dailey, & Lou Berberet |
| Fielding Average | 1.000 | Same as above |

Career Fielding Records-Catcher 1946-65

| Putouts 8,711 | 5 | John Roseboro |
| Total Chances 9,619 | 5 | John Roseboro |

World Series Records

7-Game Series Fielding Records-Catcher

| 1952 Putouts | 59 | 6 | Self |
| 1958 Putouts | 60 | 10 | Tim McCarver |

Career Batting Records 1946-65

Games Played	75		Never broken
At Bats	259		Never broken
Hits	71		Never broken
Singles	49		Never broken
Doubles	10		Tied Frankie Frisch
Runs Scored	41	1	Mickey Mantle
RBIs	39	1	Mickey Mantle
Total Bases	117	1	Mickey Mantle
Extra Base Hits	22	1	Mickey Mantle
Series Played	14		Never broken

New York Yankee Club Records

Season Fielding Records-Catcher

1951	Double Plays 25			Never broken
1956	Putouts 732	8		Elston Howard
1958	Fewest Errors	0		Never broken
	Fielding Average	1.000		Never broken

Career Fielding Records-Catcher 1946-65

Most Years	18		Never broken
Putouts	8,711		Never broken
Fewest Errors			
Per Year	7 . 8	4	Elston Howard
Double Plays	17 5		Never broken
Total Chances	9, 619		Never broken
Fielding Average	.988	4	Elston Howard

Summary

Yogi Berra has broken three of Babe Ruth's records. All three are in the category of World Series career batting records. The Babe played in 10 World Series and that record would last 31 years before Yogi Berra would play in his 11th fall classic. Yogi went on to play in 14 World Series, a feat that no other player in baseball has ever done.

The Bambino scored 37 runs in World Series games and Yogi broke this mark with 41 runs. The Babe had 96 total bases, but Berra bested this by compiled 117 total bases.

Yogi created 32 marks in all, his most impressive being in the World Series. He was a tremendous clutch hitter and pitchers feared him because Yogi would swing at any pitch he could reach. Unlike Ted Williams, Berra, by all standards, had a terrible strike zone. He did not think to himself, "Is the ball in the strike zone?" before he decided to swing. His thought was always, "Can I hit it?" regardless where the pitch was.

From the positive results Yogi had during his career, the answer that must have kept coming into his mind was,

"Yes, I can hit this pitch." He was so successful with his hitting philosophy that he established ten career batting records in the World Series. Six of them have never been broken and four have only been broken by Mickey Mantle.

Overlooked in Berra's career was his outstanding talents as a catcher. When he came up to the big leagues he was primarily an outfielder and not a very good one at that. Fortunately the Yankees had a coach by the name of Bill Dickey and he worked magic with Yogi, turning him into one of the game's best catchers. This was a wonderful surprise to the Yankees and perhaps to Berra himself. Casey Stengel once said of Yogi, "He looks funny in a baseball suit." He certainly did not have the body of a typical catcher. Berry was short, squat and clumsy. But Yogi fooled them all, or perhaps Dickey was simply a genius. Nevertheless, Berra's improvement was phenomenal and quick. Even though he didn't look it, he was quick with his feet and quick in his reactions. He pounced on bunted balls and easily threw out runners going to first or trying for second. He had no problem throwing out runners attempting to steal bases. And was he ever a sure-handed receiver! In 1958, he surprised the baseball world by going through a full season without making an error. The Yankees have had many outstanding catchers but none have been able to duplicate Berra's feat. So outstanding was Berra defensively, that he led the league a remarkable 30 times in various fielding departments. Only Gabby Hartnett had as many league leading titles as a catcher.

Berra's talents and value to the New York Yankees did not go unnoticed. Three times he was voted the MVP, and this was despite Mickey Mantle's commanding presence.

Yogi was a model of consistency. He was always batting around the .300 mark and belted 20 or more home runs for ten consecutive years and when he retired he had hit more home runs than any previous catcher. He was most difficult to strikeout as can be seen by his marvelous home run to strikeout ratio. He hit 358 homers and only went down on strikes 415 times. This is one of the lowest ratios in baseball. (Joe DiMaggio hit 369 homers and whiffed 369 times.) Yogi Berra became a Hall of Famer in 1971.

Post season Awards

1951 MVP
1954 MVP
1955 MVP

Career Statistics

Years: 19	Home Runs: 358
Strikeouts: 415	Games: 2,120
Home Run %: 4.7	Batting Ave.: .285
At Bats: 7,555	Runs Scored: 1,175
Slugging Average: .482	Hits: 2,150
RBIs: 1,430	Pinch Hit At Bats: 178
Doubles: 321	Walks: 704
Pinch Hits: 44	Triples: 49
Stolen Bases: 30	

Quotes From Yogi Berra

"Bill Dickey is learning me his experience."

"It ain't over till it's over."

"So I'm ugly. I never saw anyone hit with his face."

"We made too many wrong mistakes."

"If you ain't got a bull pen, you ain't got nuthin."

RECORD PROFILE

ALOYSIUS HARRY SIMMONS

(Al, Bucketfoot)
b. May 22, 1902, d. May 24, 1956
Phi–AL 1924-32, Chi–Al 1933-35, Det–AL 1936,
Was–AL 1937-38, Bos–NL 1939, Cin–NL 1939,
Phi–AL 1940-41, Bos–AL 1943, Phi–AL 1944

Number of Records Established-19

All-Star Game Records

Game Batting Records	Years lasted before broken		Broken by:
1933 Games Played	1	1	Self & many
1934 Games Played	2	1	Self & many
Hits	3	3	Joe Medwick
Doubles	2		Tied by Joe Medwick, Ted Kluszewski and Ernie Banks
Extra Base Hits	2		Same as above
Total Bases	5	3	Lou Gehrig
Runs Scored	3	12	Ted Williams

| 1935 Games Played | 3 | 1 | Lou Gehrig, Gabby Hartness, Ben Chapman and Charlie Gehringer |

Career Batting Records 1924-44

Games Played	3		Same as above
At Bats	13	3	Charlie Gehringer
Hits	6	3	Charlie Gehringer
Doubles	3		Tied by Joe Cronin, Ted Kluszewski, Ernie Banks Tony Oliva
Extra Base Hits	3	25	Ted Williams
Batting Average	.461	5	Ernie Lombardi
Slugging Average	.692	18	Ralph Kiner

World Series Records

Game Batting Records

| 1929 Most RBIs | 4 | 7 | Bill Dickey |

5-Game Series Batting Records

| 1929 Home Runs | 2 | 40 | Don Clendenon |
| Runs Scored | 6 | | Tied Frank Baker, Danny Murphy, Harry Hooper, and was tied by Lee May; and Boog Powell |

7-Game Series Batting Records

| 1931 Most RBIs | 8 | 25 | Mickey Mantle |

Summary

Al "Bucketfoot" Simmons spent 20 years in the outfield and one game at first base. He was a sensational hitter with a lifetime batting average of .334 and a slugging average of .535. He belted 307 homers and was a league leader in various batting categories eight times. He batted over .300 thirteen times, including eleven times in a row from 1924 to 1934. He had highs of .392, .390, .384, .381, .365 and .351.

Simmons played with seven different clubs but mostly with Connie Mack's Philadelphia Athletics. He played with such greats as Jimmie Foxx, Lefty Grove, and Mickey Cochrane. All of his 19 records were established in All-Star and World Series games. He was inducted into the Hall of Fame in 1953.

Career Statistics

Years: 20
Strikeouts: 737
Home Run %: 3.5
At Bats: 8,761
Slugging Average: .535
RBIs: 1,827
Doubles: 539
Pinch Hits: 17
Stolen Bases: 87

Home Runs: 307
Games: 2,215
Batting Average: .334
Runs Scored: 1,507
Hits: 2,927
Pinch Hit At Bats: 66
Walks: 615
Triples: 149

RECORD PROFILE

Joseph Floyd Vaughn

(Arky)
b. Mar. 9, 1912
Pit-NL 1932-41, Bkn-NL 1942-48

Number of Records Established–17

All-Star Game Records

		Years lasted before broken	Broken by:
Game Batting Records			
1937	At Bats	5 12	Pee Wee Reese
1941	Home Runs	2	Tied by Ted Williams, Al Rosen, Willie McCovey and Gary Carter
	Total Bases	9 5	Ted Williams
	Extra Base Hits	2	Tied by many
	RBIs	4 5	Ted Williams
1942	Games Played	7 1	Billy Herman
Career Batting Records 1932-48			
	Games Played	7 1	Billy Herman

Runs	5	8	Joe DiMaggio
Home Runs	2	18	Ted Williams
Total Bases	15	18	Ted Williams
Extra Base Hits	3	18	Ted Williams

Pittsburgh Pirates Club Records

Season Batting Records

1935	Home Runs	19	6	Vince DiMaggio
	Batting Average	.385		**Never broken**
	Bases On Balls	97	1	Self
1936	Bases On Balls	118	4	Elbie Fletcher

Career Fielding Records-SS 1932-41

Double Plays	791	21	Dick Groat
Fielding Average .950	21		Dick Groat

Summary

Arky Vaughn was one of the top-hitting shortstops in baseball. In a brilliant 14 year career, he batted .318 and had ten consecutive seasons of batting over .300. In all, he hit .300 or more 12 times.

Vaughn's most outstanding year was in 1935, when he slammed 192 hits, batted a league leading .385, and slugged a solid .607. He led the league in various batting departments 12 times. He was a champion in the areas of: triples (three times), runs scored, and bases on balls, and had single titles in stolen bases and batting and slugging averages.

Arky was also a fine defensive shortstop as well. He led all shortstops in fielding categories eleven times.

His most impressive records are found in All-Star games where he truly excelled. Seven times he was voted to the All-Star team and it was here that he became a Babe Ruth record breaker. When he had played his last All-Star game he was the leader in games played, runs scored, home runs, total bases, and extra base hits. It would take the great Joe DiMaggio and Ted Williams to do more offensively in All-Star games than Arky Vaughn.

Vaughn played half his career with the Pittsburgh Pirates and the balance with the Brooklyn Dodgers. While with the Pirates he established a club record in 1935 by batting .385. To this day, no Pirate player has ever broken his mark. He was voted into the Hall of Fame in 1985.

Career Statistics

Years: 14
Batting Average: .318
Home Run %: 1.4
At Bats: 6,622
Strikeouts: 276
RBIs: 926
Doubles: 356
Pinch Hits: 21
Stolen Bases: 118

Home Runs: 96
Games: 1,817
Slugging Average: .453
Runs Scored: 1,173
Hits: 2,103
Pinch Hit At Bats: 71
Walks: 937
Triples: 128

RECORD PROFILE

WILLIAM HAROLD TERRY
(Bill, Memphis Bill)
b. Oct. 30, 1898
NY-NL 1923-36

Number of Records Established–45

National League Records

	Years lasted before broken	Broken by:
Season Batting Records		
1930 Most Hits	254	**Never broken**

All-Star Game Records

Game Batting Records

1933 Games Played	1	1	Self & many
Singles	2	4	Charlie Gehringer
1934 Games Played	2	1	Self & many
1935 Games Played	3	1	Lou Gehrig, Gabby Hartnett, Ben Chapman and Charlie Gehringer

Career Batting Records 1923-36

Games Played	3	1	Same as above
Singles	4	3	Charlie Gehringer

World Series Records

7-Game Series Batting Records

1924 Batting Average	.429	1	Max Carey
Slugging Average	.786	1	Joe Harris

New York Giants Club Records

Rookie Batting Records

1924 Home Run %	3.1	21	Danny Gardella
Pinch Hit At Bats	38	3	Mel Ott
Pinch Hits	9	3	Mel Ott

Season Batting Records

1924 Pinch Hit At Bats	38	3	Mel Ott
Pinch Hits	9	3	Mel Ott
1926 Pinch Hit At Bats	38	1	Mel Ott
Pinch Hits	12	6	Sam Leslie
1929 Batting Average	.372	1	Self
1930 Batting Average	.401		Never broken
Hits	254		Never broken
Singles	177		Never broken
Total Bases	392		Never broken
1931 Doubles	43		Tied by Willie Mays

Season Fielding Records-1B

1927 Double Plays	135	1	Self
1928 Double Plays	148	24	Whitey Lockman
1930 Assists	128	2	Self
1932 Assists	137		Never broken
1935 Fewest Errors	6		Tied by Johnny Mize twice
Fielding Average	.996		Tied by Johnny Mize twice

Career Batting Records 1923-36

Games Played	],721	11	Mel Ott
At Bats	6,428	11	Mel Ott
Hits	2,193	11	Mel Ott
Singles	1,554	11	Mel Ott

Doubles	373	11	Mel Ott
Home Runs	154	11	Mel Ott
RBIs	1,078	11	Mel Ott
Extra Base Hits	639	11	Mel Ott
Total Bases	3,252	11	Mel Ott
Slugging Average	.506	11	Mel Ott
Pinch Hit At Bats	113	2	Sam Leslie
Pinch Hits	34	2	Sam Leslie

Career Fielding Records-IB 1923-36

Years	12	43	Willie McCovey
Putouts	15,625		Never broken
Assists	1,093		Never broken
Double Plays	1,303		Never broken
Total Chances	16,852		Never broken

Summary

Bill Terry compiled a lifetime batting average of .341. He was called "Memphis Bill" and he batted over .300 ten times in a row and was the last National League player to hit over .400. Terry rattled the fences for a .401 batting average way back in 1930. In the same season, he rapped 254 hits and this record has not been broken by a National League player. Six times the Giant slugger had seasons of 200 or more hits and at first base he led all first basemen in various fielding categories a fabulous 21 times. This leaves no doubt that he was a super all-round player and one of baseball's greatest first basemen.

Terry was a rookie with the Giants in 1924 and he participated in his first World Series that year. He wasted no time in setting two marvelous World Series records in batting average and slugging average for a 7-game series. Terry came to bat 14 times and rapped 6 hits which included a triple and a home run. His record batting average was a whopping .429 and his slugging mark was a hefty .786.

Terry played in three World Series with the Giants and got six hits in each series. He also drove in 7 runs and scored 7 runs while batting .295 and slugging two home runs.

Bill Terry was one of the New York Giants' greatest players of all-time. He established 36 club records of which 9 have never been broken. To this day, no Giant player has had more hits, singles, total bases or a higher batting average than his. And no Giant first baseman has recorded more putouts, assists, double plays or total chances at first base.

When he retired in 1936, he held 12 career batting records. Ten have been broken by the great Mel Ott and two by Sam Leslie. He was voted into the Hall of Fame in 1954.

Career Statistics

Years: 14

Strikeouts: 449

Home Run %: 2.4

At Bats: 6,428

Slugging Average: .506

RBIs: 1,078

Doubles: 373

Pinch Hits: 34

Stolen Bases: 56

Home Runs: 154

Games: 1,721

Batting Average: .341

Runs Scored: 1,120

Hits: 2,193

Pinch Hit At Bats: 113

Walks: 537

Triples: 112

Quotes From Bill Terry

"Brooklyn? Is Brooklyn still in the league?" (As Giants manager in 1934. His words would come back to haunt him as the lowly Dodgers beat the Giants the last two games of the season to deprive them of the pennant.)

"Baseball can survive anything." (When asked if baseball could survive the war.)

"No business in the world has made more money with poorer management."

"Baseball must be a great game to survive the fools who run it."

RECORD PROFILE

ALLIE PIERCE REYNOLDS

(Superchief)
b. Feb. 10, 1915
Cle-AL 1942-46, NY-AL 1947-54

Number of Records Established-15

World Series Pitching Records

	Years lasted before broken	Broken by:
5-Game Series Records (Mix. 10 Innings)		
1949 Fewest Hits 2		**Never broken**
6-Game Series Records (Mix. 10 Innings)		
1953 Games Pitched 3	6	Larry Sherry
Saves 1	6	Larry Sherry
Bases On Balls 11		Tied Lefty Tyler & Lefty Gomez
7-Game Series Records (Mix. 10 Innings)		
1952 Shutouts	1 5	Lew Burdette
Career Pitching Records 1942-54		
Wins	7 11	Whitey Ford
Games Pitched	15 11	Whitey Ford

Bases On Balls	32	11	Whitey Ford
Strikeouts	62	11	Whitey Ford
Saves	4	21	Rollie Fingers

Cleveland Indians Club Records

Rookie Pitching Records

1943 Strikeouts 151	12		Herb Score
Relief Losses	6	18	Frank Funk

New York Yankee Club Records

Season Pitching Records

1951 Most No-Hitters	1	Tied Tom Hughes, Sam Jones & Monte Pearson
1951 Most No-Hitters	2	**Never broken**

Career Pitching Records

1947-54	No-Hitters	2	**Never broken**

Summary

They called him "Superchief" because he was both super and an Indian. Allie Reynolds was an outstanding pitcher. He possessed a blazing fast ball and an extreme desire to win. He was a fierce competitor and came out on top most of the time. His career results are 182 wins and 107 losses. This represents a super winning percentage of .630. Although not in the Hall of Fame, these two statistics would place him above 50 per cent of the pitchers who are in the Hall.

Reynolds began his career with a second division Cleveland Indians and did well in his 5 years there. He came to the Yankees in 1947 and with a first division club did even better. In eight years with the Yankees he never had a losing season. For his first six years he was considered the ace of the staff. During that span he averaged 17.5 wins a year. He enjoyed his best season in 1952 when he won 20 and lost only eight.

The "Superchief" was not only a Yankee leader but a league leader. Seven times he was the best of all American League pitchers. As a rookie in 1943, he struck out more batters than all the veteran pitchers. He again won this crown in 1952 while also leading the league in shutouts. He also led the league in shutouts in 1951, in ERA in 1952, and winning percentage in 1947.

In six of his eight years with the Yankees, Reynolds led them to pennants and World Series victories. He is one of the most successful pitchers in World Series history. He appeared in 15 games which places him 3rd, started 9 games (6th), completed 5 games (10th), hurled 77.1 innings (8th), struck out 62 (3rd), tossed two shutouts (4th), won two games in relief (2nd), had 4 saves (2nd) and in all, won 7 games which places him on the all-time list behind Whitey Ford. He had a fine winning percentage of .778 and ERA of 2.79.

Reynolds established 15 records during his successful career. Two of them that he most cherishes are for most no-hitters in one season, when he pitched two in 1951, and in the 1949 World Series, when in that 5-games series, he allowed only 2 hits in 12.1 innings, which broke the previous record held by Babe Ruth. Also, in those 12.1 innings, he struck out 14 batters.

Career Statistics

Years: 13	Wins: 182
Losses: 107	Winning %: .630
ERA: 3.30	Games: 434
Starts: 309	Completions: 137
Innings: 2,492.1	Hits: 2,193
Walks: 1,261	Strikeouts: 1,423
Shutouts: 36	Relief Wins: 18
Relief Losses: 19	Saves: 49

RECORD PROFILE

EARLE BRYAN COMBS
(The Kentucky Colonel)
b. May 14, 1899, d. July 21, 1976

Number of Records Established—42

National League Records

		Years lasted before broken	Broken by:
Rookie Fielding Records-CF			
1925 Putouts	401	5	Tommy Oliver
Total Chances	422	2	Alex Metzler
Fielding Average	.979	5	Tommy Oliver

World Series Records

Game Batting Records			
1932 Runs Scored	4		Tied Babe Ruth and was tied by Frank Crosetti and Reggie Jackson
4-Game Series Batting Records			
1926 Runs Scored	6	2	Babe Ruth
4-Game Series Fielding Records-CF			
1927 Putouts	16		**Never broken**
Career Fielding Records-CF 1924-35			
Chances w/o Errors	43	19	Joe DiMaggio

New York Yankee Club Records

Rookie Batting Records

1925	Games Played	150	1	Tony Lazzeri
	At Bats	593	1	Mark Keonig
	Hits	203	11	Joe DiMaggio
	Singles	151		**Never broken**
	Triples	13	1	Tony Lazzeri
	Runs Scored	117	11	Joe DiMaggio
	Total Bases	274	11	Joe DiMaggio

Rookie Fielding Records-CF

1925	Putouts	401		**Never broken**
	Fewest Errors	9		Tied by Bobby Brown
	Total Chances/game	2,8		**Never broken**
	Total Chances	422		**Never broken**
	Fielding Average	.979		**Never broken**

Season Batting Records

1927	At Bats	648	12	Frank Crosetti
	Hits	231	59	Don Mattingly
	Singles	166		Tied Willie Keeler
	Triples	23		**Never broken**
1931	Longest Hitting Streak	29	10	Joe DiMaggio

Season Fielding Records-CF

1925	Putouts	401	2	Self
	Total Chances/game	2.8	2	Self
	Total Chances	422	2	Self
1927	Putouts	411	1	Self
	Total Chances/game	2.8	1	Self
	Total Chances	431	1	Self
1928	Putouts	424	16	Johnny Lindell
	Double Plays	7		Tied Ray Demmitt, was tied by Ben Chapman
	Total Chances game	3.0	16	Johnny Lindell
	Total Chances	444	9	Joe DiMaggio

Career Batting Records 1924-35

	Triples	154	4	Lou Gehrig

Career Fielding Records-CF 1924-35

Putouts	2,874	16	Joe DiMaggio
Assists	61	16	Joe DiMaggio
Errors	84	16	Joe DiMaggio
Fewest Errors per year	9.3	16	Joe DiMaggio
Total Chances/game	2.7	16	Joe DiMaggio
Total Chances	3,019	16	Joe DiMaggio
Double Plays	22	16	Joe DiMaggio

Summary

Earle Combs was a charter member of the New York Yankees' "Murderers' Row." He was an exciting player who could do it all. He could run, throw, catch, and hit with exceptional abilities, as can be seen by his lifetime .325 batting average and his host of fielding records. He had tremendous speed that he used well to cover the vast center field area in Yankee stadium. His exceptional speed also helped him to compile 154 triples, a record that only Lou Gehrig has broken. The swift moving centerfielder has six unbroken Yankee club records to his credit. As a rookie, no Yankee has ever hit more singles, fielded more putouts in center field, had more total chances per game, total chances or a higher fielding average. In 1927, Combs used his outstanding speed to reach third base safely on 23 triples, a record which still stands today. He was elected into the Hall of Fame in 1970.

Career Statistics

Years: 12
Strikeouts: 278
Home Run %: 1.0
At Bats: 5,748
Slugging Average: 462
RBIs: 629
Doubles: 309
Pinch Hits: 17
Stolen Bases: 96

Home Runs: 58
Games: 1,454
Batting Average: .325
Runs Scored: 1,186
Hits: 1,866
Pinch Hit At Bats: 56
Walks: 670
Triples: 154

RECORD PROFILE

HAROLD JOSEPH TRAYNOR
(Pie, Pie Man)
b. Nov. 11, 1899, d. Mar. 16, 1972
Pit-NL 1920-37

Number of Records Established–32

National League Records

	Years lasted before broken		Broken by:
Season Fielding Records-3B			
1925 Double Plays	41	25	Hank Thompson
Career Fielding Records-3B 1920-37			
Games Played	1,864	31	Eddie Mathews
Putouts	2,291		**Never broken**
Assists	3,525	31	Eddie Mathews
Double Plays	308	31	Eddie Mathews
Total Chances	6,140	31	Eddie Mathews

Major League Records

Season Fielding Records-3B			
1925 Double Plays	41	2	Sammy Hale

Career Fielding Records-3B 1920-37

Games Played	1,864	25	Eddie Yost
Double Plays	308	25	Eddie Yost

All-Star Game Records

Game Batting Records

1933	Games Played	1	1	Self & many
	Doubles	1	1	Al Simmons
	Extra Base Hits	1	1	Al Simmons
1934	Games Played	2	1	Self & many
	Singles	2	3	Charlie Gehringer
1935	Games Played	3	1	Lou Gehrig, Ben Chapman, Gabby Hartnett, and Charlie Gehringer

Career Batting Records 1920-37

Games Played	3	1	Lou Gehrig, Ben Chapman, Gabby Hartnett, and Charlie Gehringer

World Series Records

4-Game Series Fielding Records-3B

1927 Errors	1	11	Red Rolfe

7-Game Series Batting Records

1925 Triples	2	22	Billy Johnson

7-Game Series Fielding Records-3B

1925 Assists	18	15	Pinky Higgins

Pittsburgh Pirates Club Records

Rookie Fielding Records-3B

1922 Double Plays	19	27	Pete Castiglione

Season Fielding Records-3B

1923 Double Plays	30	1	Self

1924	Double Plays	31	1	Self
	Fewest Errors	14	11	Tommy Thevenow
	Fielding Average	.968	38	Dick Hoak
1925	Double Plays	41		**Never broken**

Career Fielding Records-3B 1920-37

Years	14		**Never broken**
Putouts	2,286		**Never broken**
Assists	3,509		**Never broken**
Errors	323		**Never broken**
Double Plays	308		**Never broken**
Total Chances	6,118		**Never broken**
Fielding Average	.944	27	Dick Hoak

Summary

Pie Traynor or Brooks Robinson. . . one of these players was probably the finest third baseman the game has ever seen. During his era, Pie Traynor was heads and shoulders above his peers at the hot corner, according to all who saw him. To prove it, all one has to do is look up the number of times he led the league in various fielding categories. The total comes to a resounding 25 times.

He was called the "Pie Man," and boy could he hit. For 17 years, he averaged batting a solid .320. In a 12-year span, he batted over .300 ten times and had super highs of .366, .356, and .342. In 1923, he won the triples crown. So good was Traynor that even in the twilight of his career he was voted to the All-Star team three years in a row. It was in this area that he eclipsed a record held by Babe Ruth.

A true test of a player's greatness is in the longevity of the records they create. Traynor was so far ahead of his time that it would take Hank Thompson 25 years to break his season doubles record. It would take Eddie Mathews 31 years to break his career fielding records for games played, assists, double plays, and total chances. But even Mathews could not break Traynor's mark for most putouts. This record still stands after more than half a century.

Pie Traynor was easily the greatest third baseman in the history of the Pittsburgh Pirates franchise. Seven of his fielding records are still unbroken in season double plays, career years, putouts, assists, errors, double plays and total chances. The fact that Traynor's fielding average record has been broken is probably due to the great improvement in gloves that modern players have the advantage of using. Traynor was inducted into the Hall of Fame in 1948.

Career Statistics

Years: 17

Strikeouts: 278

Home Run %: 0.8

At Bats: 7,559

Slugging Average: .435

RBIs: 1,273

Doubles: 371

Pinch Hits: 7

Stolen Bases: 158

Home Runs: 58

Games: 1,941

Batting Average: .320

Runs Scored: 1,183

Hits: 2,416

Pinch Hit At Bats: 24

Walks: 472

Triples: 164

RECORD PROFILE

HOWARD EARL AVERILL

(Rock)
b. May 21, 1902, d. Aug. 16, 1983
Cle-AL 1929-39, Det-AL 1939-40, Bos-NL 1941

Number of Records Established–41

All-Star Game Records

		Years lasted before broken	Broken by:
Game Batting Records			
1933	Games Played	1 1	Self & many
1934	Games Played	2 1	By many
	Triples	1 44	Rod Carew
	Total Bases	5 3	Lou Gehrig
	Extra Base Hits	2	Tied by many
	RBIs	3 3	Lou Gehrig
Career Batting Records 1929-41			
	Games Played	2 1	By many
	Doubles	1 1	Al Simmons
	Triples	1 39	Rod Carew
	Extra Base Hits	2 1	Al Simmons

Cleveland Indians Club Records

Rookie Batting Records

1929	Extra Base Hits	74	5	Hal Trosky

Rookie Fielding Records-CF

1929	Putouts	398		Never broken
	Assists	14		Never broken
	Errors	14		Never broken
	Double Plays	3	16	Felix Mackiewicz
	Total Chancesgame	2.7	16	Felix Mackiewicz
	Total Chances	416		Never broken

Season Batting Records

1931	Home Runs	32	1	Self
	Home Run %	5.1	1	Self
	Runs Scored	140		Never broken
	RBIs	43	5	Hal Trosky
	Total Bases	361	3	Hal Trosky
1932	Home Runs	32	2	Hal Trosky
	Home Run %	5.1	2	Hal Trosky

Season Fielding Records-CF

1930	Errors	19		Never broken
1931	Putouts	398	1	Self
1932	Putouts	412	47	Rick Manning
	Total Chances	440	52	Brett Butler

Career Batting Records 1929-39

	Triples	121		Never broken
	Home Runs	225		Never broken
	Home Run %	3.7	2	Hal Trosky
	Runs	1,154		Never broken
	RBIs	1,085		Never broken
	Extra Base Hits	724		Never broken
	Total Bases	3,201		Never broken
	Strikeouts	450	10	Ken Keltner
	Slugging Average	.541	2	Hal Trosky

Career Fielding Records-CF 1929-39

Years	11	Tied Tris Speaker and was tied by Larry Doby
Games	1,497	**Never broken**
Putouts	3,876	**Never broken**
Errors	121	**Never broken**

Summary

The Cleveland Indians have had many great players during the history of their franchise. In the early years it was Hall of Famers Shoeless Joe Jackson and Nap Lajoie. Then it was Hall of Famer Tris Speaker who came over from the Boston Red Sox. Earl Averill replaced Speaker in center field and went on to become one of the greatest of all Cleveland players.

Averill did well as a rookie in 1929 when he set a Cleveland record for most extra base hits and in center field he placed six new records in the book. Even though 64 years have gone by, no Cleveland rookie centerfielder has had more putouts, assists, errors or total chances.

Averill was a lifetime .318 hitter and made the All-Star team in 1933 and 1934. In these games, against the National League's greatest players, his name was entered in the record book ten times.

In his 13-year career, he batted over .300 eight times. His best season was in 1936 when he smacked enemy pitchers for a .378 average and led the league in hits with 232, in triples with 15, and had 39 doubles and 28 home runs. He also scored 136 runs and drove in 126. Averill was also a fine fielder and was a league leader in that department five times.

An interesting trivia question would be: What Cleveland player holds the career record for most triples, home runs, runs scored, RBIs, extra base hits and total bases? The answer would be Earl Averill. And in center field there has never been a Cleveland player who has played as many games or made more putouts.

Averill was inducted into the Hall of Fame in 1975

Career Statistics

Years: 13

Strikeouts: 518

Home Run %: 3.7

At Bats: 6,358

Slugging Average: .533

RBIs: 1,165

Doubles: 401

Pinch Hits: 22

Stolen Bases: 69

Home Runs: 238

Games: 1,619

Batting Average: .318

Runs Scored: 1,224

Hits: 2,020

Pinch Hit At Bats: 73

Walks: 775

Triples: 128

RECORD PROFILE

PAUL GLEE WANER
(Big Poison)
b. Apr. 16, 1903, d. Aug. 29, 1965
Pit-NL 1926-40, Bkn-NL 1941, Bos-NL 1941-42,
Bkn-NL 1943-44, NE-AL 1944-45

Number of Records Established–39

National League Records

	Years lasted before broken		Broken by:
Rookie Fielding Records-RF			
1926 Putouts	307	9	Ival Goodman
Season Batting Records			
1932 Doubles	62	4	Joe Medwick
Career Fielding Records-RF 1926-44			
Games Played	2,179	2	Mel Ott
Putouts	4,631		**Never broken**
Putouts/game	2.1		**Never broken**
Total Chances	4,968		**Never broken**
Fielding Ave.	.975	2	Mel Ott

Major League Records

Rookie Fielding Records-RF

1926 Putouts	307	9	Ival Goodman

Career Fielding Records-RF 1926-44

Putouts	4,631	29	Al Kaline
Total Chances/game	2.1		Tied by Al Kaline
Total Chances	4,968	29	Al Kaline

All-Star Game Records

Game Batting Records

1933 Games Played	1	1	Self & many
1934 Games Played	2	1	Self & many
1935 Games Played	3	1	Lou Gehrig, Charlie Gehringer, Gabby Hartnett and Ben Chapman
1937 At Bats	5	12	PeeWee Reese

Career Batting Records 1926-45

Games Played	3	1	Lou Gehrig, Charlie Gehringer, Gabby Hartnett and Ben Chapman

Pittsburgh Pirates Club Records

Rookie Batting Records

1926 Doubles	35	Never broken
Extra Base Hits	65	Never broken

Rookie Fielding Records-RF

1926 Putouts	307		Never broken
Assists	21		Never broken
Total Chances/game	2.4		Never broken
Total Chances	336		Never broken
Fielding Ave.	.976	14	Bob Elliott

Season Batting Records

1927	Hits	237		Never broken
	Singles	171	1	Lloyd Waner
	RBIs	131		Never broken
1928	Doubles	50	4	Self
1932	Doubles	62		Never broken

Season Fielding Records-RF

1927	Total Chances/game	2.5	4	Kiwi Cuyler
1930	Total Chances/game	2.6	1	Self
1931	Total Chances/game	2.7		Tied Jimmy Barrett and Dave Parker
1932	Putouts	367	12	Jimmy Barrett

Career Batting Records 1926-40

	Home Runs	108	13	Ralph Kiner

Career Fielding Records-RF 1926-40

	Years	15	32	Roberto Clemente
	Putouts	4411	32	Roberto Clemente
	Assists	221	32	Roberto Clemente
	Double Plays		46	Never broken
	Total Chances	4747	32	Roberto Clemente
	Fielding Average	.976	5	Jimmy Barrett

Summary

"Big Poison" stood only 5'8 " and weighed all of 153 pounds, which made him about the same size as his younger brother, Lloyd who was called "Little Poison."

Paul Waner had a super 20-year career and was one of those rare hitters who compiled more than 3,000 hits. In all, he had 3,152 to go along with a splendid lifetime batting average of .333. He was a league leader in various batting categories 13 times. He batted over .300 his first 12 seasons in a row, and added two more .300 plus seasons later in his career. He had averages of .380, .373, .370, .368, .362

and .354. He belted 200 or more hits in a season eight times and was a two-time hits champion.

Waner also won two titles in doubles, triples, and runs scored and was a three-time batting average champion.

He played most of his career with the Pittsburgh Pirates and is proud of having 10 club records which have never been broken in more than half a century.

His rookie doubles and extra base hit records remain unbroken for more than 67 years, as are his rookie fielding records for right fielders in putouts, assists, total chances per game and total chances.

In 1927 he slammed 237 hits, and had 131 RBIs, and these marks have never been broken. In 1928, the tough little slugger belted 50 doubles to set a new mark which he broke himself in 1932 with 62. To this day, no Pirate player has had more doubles in one season.

Although he was a small man by today's comparisons, Waner had plenty of power and when he left the Pirates in 1940 he had hit more home runs than any previous player. This mark stood 13 years before Ralph Kiner would become the all-time Pirate home run king.

When Waner left the club in 1940, he also had more putouts, assists, double plays, total chances and highest fielding average of any Pirate right fielder. His double play record still has not been broken, although Roberto Clemente eventually broke most of his other marks.

Career Statistics

Years: 20
Strikeouts: 376
Home Run %: 1.2
At Bats: 9,459
Slugging Average: .473
RBIs: 1,309
Doubles: 603
Pinch Hits: 40
Stolen Bases: 104

Home Runs: 112
Games: 2,549
Batting Average: .333
Runs Scored: 1,626
Hits: 3,152
Pinch Hit At Bats: 164
Bases On Balls: 1,091
Triples: 190

RECORD PROFILE

ANTHONY MICHAEL LAZZARI

(Poosh 'Em Up)
b. Dec. 6, 1903, d. Aug. 6, 1946
NY-AL 1926-37, Chi-NL 1938, Bkn-NL 1939, NY-NL 1939

Number of Records Established–29

American League Records

	Years lasted before broken	Broken by:
Rookie Batting Records		
1926 RBIs	114 3	Dale Alexander
Strikeouts	96 6	Bruce Campbell
Rookie Fielding Records-2B		
1926 Assists	461 2	Carl Lind
Double Plays	72 2	Carl Lind

Major League Batting Records

Rookie Batting Records

1926 Strikeouts	96	6	Bruce Campbell

New York Yankees Club Records

Rookie Batting Records

1926 Games Played	155	36	Tom Tresh
Triples	14	10	Joe DiMaggio
RBIs	114	10	Joe DiMaggio
Strikeouts	96	43	Bobby Mercer

Rookie Fielding Records-2B

1926 Putouts	298	50	Willie Randolph
Assists	461		**Never broken**
Errors	31		Tied by Joe Gordon
Double Plays	72	12	Joe Gordon
Total Chances	790		**Never broken**
Fielding Average	.961	23	Jerry Coleman

Season Batting Records

1926 Strikeouts	96	11	Frank Crosetti

Season Fielding Records-2B

1929 Double Plays	101	10	Joe Gordon

Career Fielding Records-2B 1926-37

Putouts	3,305	51	Willie Randolph
Assists	4,392	51	Willie Randolph
Errors	257		**Never broken**
Double Plays	797	29	Bobby Richardson
Total Chances	7,954	51	Willie Randolph

World Series Records

Game Batting Records

1936 RBIs	5	24	Bobby Richardson

4-Game Series Fielding Records-2B

1927 Putouts	10	11	Joe Gordon

	Assists	18	**Never broken**
	Errors	1 1	Self
1928	Errors	2	Tied by Joe Gordon and Billy Herman

American League Records (Cont'd)

Game Batting Records

1936	RBIs	11	**Never broken**
	Cons. Game RBIs	15	**Never broken**

Major League Records (Cont'd)

1936	Cons. Game RBIs	15	**Never broken**

Summary

Imagine playing a baseball career having teammates like Babe Ruth, Lou Gehrig and Joe DiMaggio. Tony Lazzeri was another lucky major leaguer to enjoy such an honor. But they were lucky to have him as well, especially in a 1936 game when the powerful Yankee second baseman astounded the baseball world by driving in 11 runs in one game. He accomplished this by coming to the plate with the bases loaded three times. Twice he hit home runs and another time he tripled. Babe Ruth was gone and didn't have the thrill of seeing Lazzeri's great feat, but Joe DiMaggio was there in awe as a rookie. Lou Gehrig also witnessed this great day. Lazzeri would go on to knock in four more runs in the following game to set a major league record of 15 RBIs, in two consecutive games. This phenomenal record still stands. The one game RBI major league record is 12 held by Jim Bottomley in 1924.

Tony Lazzeri had many outstanding days and seasons with the Yankees. Another such day was in the 1936 World Series when he broke Babe Ruth's record of 4 RBIs, in one game. In that series both he and Bill Dickey would drive in 5 runs in one game to take away another of Babe Ruth's records. Lazzeri and Dickey held onto their records for 24 years until another second baseman, Bobby

Richardson, would lay claim to a new record by batting in six runs in one World Series game.

Lazzeri, who recently was inducted into the Hall of Fame, made his presence known immediately upon his arrival to the big leagues. In his rookie year of 1926, he belted 162 hits of which 18 were home runs, 28 doubles and 14 triples. He scored 79 runs and drove in 114 to establish a new American League rookie RBI record.

"Poosh 'Em Up" Tony was just as good with the glove as he was with the bat. He also created American League rookie records for most assists and double plays for a second baseman. The assists mark remains a Yankee club record that has never been broken and it contributed to 790 total chances, which is also an unbroken Yankee record. Lazzeri also claims an unbroken World Series fielding record when in 1927 he posted 18 assists in a 4-game series for a second baseman.

He was of Italian descent, stood 5'112" and weighed only 170 pounds, but he was all muscle and all scrap, likened to a more modern Yankee second baseman by the name of Billy Martin. Lazzeri used his 170 pounds well by blasting home runs in double figures 10 times during the 12-years he proudly wore the Yankee pin stripes. Five times he batted over .300 with a high of .354 in 1929. Seven times he drove in 100 or more runs.

Career Statistics

Years: 14

Strikeouts: 864

Home Run %: 2.8

At Bats: 6,297

Slugging Average: 467

RBIs: 1,191

Doubles: 334

Pinch Hits: 13

Stolen Bases: 148

Home Runs: 178

Games: 1,739

Batting Average: .292

Runs Scored: 986

Hits: 1,840

Pinch Hit At Bats: 38

Walks: 870

Triples: 115

BIBLIOGRAPHY

Murray, Tom
SPORT Magazine's All-Time All-Stars
New York: Atheneum, 1977

Reichler, Joseph L., ed.
The Baseball Encyclopedia:
The Complete & Official Record of Major League Baseball
New York: Macmillan, 1987

Seymour, Harold
Baseball: TheEarly Years
Toronto: Oxford Universitv Press, 1960

Carter, Craig, ed.
The Complete Baseball Record Book
St. Louis, Missouri: The Sporting News, 1987

Siwoff, Seymour
The Book of Baseball Records
New York: Sterling, 1981

Smith, Robert
The Pioneers of Baseball
Boston: Little, Brown & Co., 1978

Turkin, Hy, and S. C. Thompson
The Official Encyclopedia of Baseball, 10th edition
South Brunswick, NJ.: A. S. Barnes, 1979

Kal Wagenheim
Babe Ruth. . . His Life & Legend
Waterfront Press, Maplewood,
N.J. 1990

Photo Credits

The following teams have donated many photographs found in this book. I would like to thank the Los Angeles Dodgers, Philadelphia Phillies, New York Yankees, San Francisco Giants, St. Louis Cardinals, Detroit Tigers, Boston Red Sox and Pittsburgh Pirates.

For other contributions, I would like to thank the Baseball Hall of Fame, Codie's Collectables, Chris Dunham Collections and JM Baseball Record Profile Collections.

I would also like to thank the following individual players who donated their photos. They are: Yogi Berra, Mickey Mantle, Roger Maris, Joe DiMaggio, Johnny Mize, Bill Dickey, Reggie Jackson, and Whitey Ford.

New S.P.I. Bestselling Baseball Books

A Day In the Season of the L.A. Dodgers

☐ All baseball lovers, and especially Dodger fans, will delight in this intimate visit to Dodger Stadium. There are photographs, interviews and descriptions of all the people and places that turn on the magic at this premier big league ballpark.

The reader not only meets big name baseball personalities like manager Tommy Lasorda and stars like Darryl Strawberry and Orel Hersheiser, but also fans, announcers, grounds crew and concession salespeople.

We meet both the guy who throws peanut bags in the stands and the one who throws curveballs in batting practice. Even a season ticket holder will have plenty to learn and love in this ode to the American pastime.

(ISBN 1-56171-084-9)

New York Yankee Records

❏ Endless delight for fans of baseball and the legendary Bronx bombers.

* Who led the Yankees in wins, E.R.A. and strikeouts in the year of your birth?

* What nine Yankee rookie records are held by Joe DiMaggio?

* Who played more seasons for the Yankees: Mickey Mantle, Lou Gehrig or Yogi Berra?

* Which Yankees performed the best during World Series, playoffs and All-Star games?

* Can you name the Yankee batting stars who also led in fielding percentage, most putouts and double plays?

All the answers are in this book, along with rare photographs, player profiles and full stats.

A superb gift for the legions of sports fans.

(ISBN 1-56171-215-9)

Boston Red Sox Records

☐ Facts and fascination for faithful Fenway fans. Here is the complete record of the best of the Bosox in their long, glorious and, yes, heartbreaking, history.

With this book in hand the reader will know:

* When the Red Sox last had two no-hitters in one season.

* In what category Fred Lynn bested Ted Williams.

* How relievers like Reardon compare to Dick "the Monster" Radatz.

* Which few right-handers won Boston's 18 batting crowns.

* What season batting records of Tris Speaker's still stand.

* Who led in errors, put-outs, strikeouts, doubles and more in every season the team has played.

(ISBN 1-56171-222-1)

To order in North America, please sent this coupon to: **S.P.I. Books** •136 W 22nd St. • New York, NY 10011 • Tel: 212/633-2022 • Fax: 212/633-2123

Please send European orders with £ payment to:
Bookpoint Ltd. • 39 Milton Park • Abingdon Oxon OX14 4TD • England • Tel: (0235) 8335001 • Fax: (0235) 861038

Please send____books. I have enclosed check or money order for $4.99 U.S./£3.50 ST.____(please add $1.95 U.S./£ for first book for postage/handling & 50¢/50p. for each additional book). Make dollar checks drawn on U.S. branches payable to **S.P.I. Books**; Sterling checks to **Bookpoint Ltd**. Allow 2 to 3 weeks for delivery.

___MC ___ Visa # _____

Exp. date _____

Name _____

Address _____

Major League Baseball Records

❏ This season-by-season rundown of major league records offers endless fascination for baseball fans. No trivia quiz can stump the reader now, with the stats
and stories of thousands of major leaguers at one's fingertips.The reader will
be able to answer (or ask) questions like these:

*   Who is the only National Leaguer to lead the circuit in hits seven times?

*   What is the record for most doubles in a season?

*   Can you name the three pitchers behind Cy Young in career wins?

*   Has anyone topped Ted Williams 1939 record of 107 walks.

*   Who managed the American league team that won the pennant by 23
     games?

* What season batting records of Tris Speaker's still stand.

All the stats are supplemented with stories, analysis and rare photos.

(ISBN 1-56171-224-8)

To order in North America, please sent this coupon to: **S.P.I. Books** •136 W 22nd St. • New York, NY 10011 •
Tel: 212/633-2022 • Fax: 212/633-2123

Please send European orders with £ payment to:
Bookpoint Ltd. • 39 Milton Park • Abingdon Oxon OX14 4TD • England • Tel: (0235) 8335001 • Fax: (0235) 861038

Please send____books. I have enclosed check or money order for $11.99 U.S./£7.50 ST.____(please add $1.95 U.S./£ for
first book for postage/handling & 50¢/50p. for each additional book). Make dollar checks drawn on U.S. branches payable to
S.P.I. Books; Sterling checks to **Bookpoint Ltd.** Allow 2 to 3 weeks for delivery.

___MC ___ Visa # _____

Exp. date _____

Name _____

Address _____

Official Profiles of Baseball Hall of Famers

❐ All of baseball's greatest hitters, pitchers, fielders, rookies and managers are profiled in this one-of-a-kind new book. You not only get their season-by-season and total career records, you even get their birthdays and nicknames.

Want to ask or answer some tough trivia questions about Hall of Fame pitchers like Lefty Groove, Don Drysdale or Whitey Ford? Do you want to compare the home run records of Hank Aaron, Babe Ruth and Harmon Killebrew? The answeres are all here.

Perhaps you want to see what chance your favorite player has of getting into the Hall of Fame, Now you can easily compare Roger Clemens' strikeout records to those of Koufax. Stack up Cecil Fielder's slugging percentage against Stan Musial, and see if Ozzie Smith's fielding records put him on a par with Brooks Robinson.

Guarantees endless fascination for the baseball fan.

(ISBN 1-56171-216-7)

To order in North America, please sent this coupon to: **S.P.I. Books** •136 W 22nd St. • New York, NY 10011 • Tel: 212/633-2022 • Fax: 212/633-2123

Please send European orders with £ payment to:
Bookpoint Ltd. • 39 Milton Park • Abingdon Oxon OX14 4TD • England • Tel: (0235) 8335001 • Fax: (0235) 861038

Please send____books. I have enclosed check or money order for $10.99 U.S./£6.99 ST.____(please add $1.95 U.S./£ for first book for postage/handling & 50¢/50p. for each additional book). Make dollar checks drawn on U.S. branches payable to **S.P.I. Books**; Sterling checks to **Bookpoint Ltd**. Allow 2 to 3 weeks for delivery.

____MC ___ Visa # _____

Exp. date _____

Name _____

Address _____